Hussein Ela

THE GLOBAL FINANCIAL CRISIS AND THE ISLAMIC FINANCE

Table of contacts

I. INTRODUCTION

The world economy is still suffering the crisis, considered the most severe since the Great Depression, where economic downturn at historic magnitude and many countries across the globe, irrespective of their development level, are still under strain dealing with this crisis.

The severe global crisis that has spilled from the financial sector to the real economy, including international trade in manufactures, commodities and services. The onset of the present crisis can be traced back to July 2007 with the liquidity crisis due to the loss of confidence in the mortgage credit markets in the United States. At first, there was uncertainty about the possible spillovers to the rest of the economy, and there was also discussion about the risks of contagion and decoupling, that is to say, the capacity of other countries – especially developing countries – to isolate themselves from the problems originating in the United States (which is the largest market for many countries). The hope was that the crisis would be restricted to financial markets, with few repercussions on the real economy and the rest of the world. This hope was shattered in September 2008 as the crisis entered an acute phase, with strong downward fluctuations in the stock markets, substantially reduced rates of economic growth, volatile exchange rates, and squeezes in demand and consumption, leading to falls in industrial production and decreasing flows of international trade and FDI, and causing impacts on related areas such as transfer of technology. The crisis has also been accompanied by increases in unemployment, with concomitant declining incomes and demand.

The severity of the current crisis has led to the evaluation of the foundations of the capitalist financial system and the search for ideas and solutions. In addition, reflects problems that go beyond the conduct of monetary policy and regulation of the financial sector. It also involves deeper inadequacies in areas such as corporate governance and competition policies. Many of these failings, in turn, have been supported by a flawed understanding of the functioning of markets, which also contributed to the recent drive towards financial deregulation. These views have been the basis for the design of policies advocated by some of the international economic institutions, and for much of the architecture of globalization.

Nobel Prize Winner, French economist Maurice Allais believes that the way out of such crises is best achieved through structural reforms through, adjusting the rate of interest to 0% and revising the tax rate to about 2%. Islamic economists belief that this is the core elements of Islamic economics. Moreover, they contend that Islamic Finance has an alternative that would prevent the recurrence of a similar crisis. Wherever the Islamic Finance is the only example of a financial system directly based on the ethical precepts of a major religion, providing not only investment guidelines but also a set of unique investment and financing products." Islamic Finance is based on Shari'ah, the Islamic law that provides guidelines for multiple aspects of Muslim life, including religion, politics, economics, banking,business and aspects of the legal system What Shari'ah compliant financing (SCF) seeks to do is to shape financial practices and accompanying legal instruments that conform to Islamic law. Major financial principles of Shari'ah include a ban on interest, a ban on uncertainty, adherence to risk-sharing and profit- sharing, promotion of ethical investments that enhance society and do not violate practices banned in the Qur'an and tangible asset- backing.

Money, according to Islamic teachings is a measure of value,not a commodity. Debt is a relationship in which risk and responsibility are shared by all parties to a contract.

Two developments that have been critical to the expansion of Islamic financial markets. In 1998, the so-called "Dow Jones Islamic Indexes fatwa" played a transformative role because it opened the door to a limited degree of "permissible impurity" in financial transactions and institutionalized a notion of cleansing and purification whereby small amounts of impermissible interest income could be cleansed or purified by donation to charity. In turn, this led to a series of equity investment tests that could be used to evaluate potential investments for Shari'ah compliance.

A second critical innovation was the introduction of sukuk – a Shari'ah compliant substitute for bonds – where capital protection is achieved not as a loan but as a binding agreement by the issuer to repurchase certain assets over a period of time.

Sukuk has now become one of the backbones of Islamic capital markets and has enabled the rapid growth of Islamic financial transactions.

The multiple reasons for the growth of the Islamic financial sector in recent years: (1) the flow of funds into Muslim oil-producing states;(2) growing political and social desire in the Muslim world for financial alternatives to banking and investment institutions that have been historically dominated by the West; (3) the spreading credit crisis in global financial markets and the need to access new sources of investment capital; (4) the growth of sovereign wealth funds and the desire to have shari'ah compliant instruments through which to invest them; and, (5) the rapidly accelerating number of cross-border multi-jurisdictional financial transactions that are possible and required in a globalized world economy Assets held by Muslim investors worldwide now exceed $1.6 trillion, and that amount is expected to grow to $2.7 trillion by 2010. Shari'ah compliant finance has become an accepted and vibrant element in international financial transactions. It offers a fresh opportunity to emphasize the moral and ethical aspects of business and finance that reaches beyond the Arab and Islamic worlds to prompt a reexamination of the core values underlying all global financial transactions – making available the financial resources needed to develop the human capital that will sustain economic and social progress.

While some have proposed that the Islamic Finance

serves as a vehicle for recovering from the international financial crisis and The Islamic banking industry may be able to strengthen its position in the international market as investors and companies seek alternate sources of financing. Other economists have argued that Islamic Finance, is a different way of structuring financial dealings; but, it is not a totally different financial system.

This book tries to note the main causes and the impacts of the current financial and economic crisis. In addition to discuss the belief that the Islamic Finance and its prospective is a viable alternative to the ailing global financial system.

II. FUNDAMENTALS OF THE ISLAMIC FINANCE

A. Islamic Economy

Islam is a comprehensive way of life, which strikes the balance between the spiritual and the material need of human being. One of the important aspects in human life is the need for a comprehensive system in order to govern their life and to ensure all the needs are catered adequately including the material needs such as the financial management. This aspect of life is closely related to the fast growing industry in the world nowadays, which is the Islamic financial services industry.

An Islamic economy is a market economy guided by moral values. Economic activities are based on principles of cooperation and responsibility. Cooperation means that an economic exchange shall be beneficial to both parties involved. Transactions in which one party wins at the expense of the other are not permissible in Islam. Thus, monopolistic dealings, usury, and exploitation are prohibited. Transactions that allow both parties to win are permissible, and these include most types of activities needed for economic prosperity .Performance-based arrangements, like profit sharing or partnership, represent the most cooperative form of beneficial agreements, and thus are highly encouraged in Islam.

Responsibility means that each individual is entitled for reward or return based on his effort and contribution. Thus gambling and lotteries are not permissible. Gambling allows an individual to gain based on pure luck, not on merit or effort. It shifts wealth blindly among participants leading to improper distribution of wealth. Gambling is a clear form of a zero-sum game where one party wins only if the other loses, and thus causes hatred and enmity among participants. A society where lotteries or gambling like activities prevail is a zero-sum society, where the winner takes all, and the rest is doomed to fail.

B. Islamic Economics

Islamic economics is a framework for studying economic activities that allow mutual benefit of exchange to be realized. It provides proper tools and techniques for evaluating economic decisions, showing when and how to achieve win/win outcomes and avoid win/lose or lose/lose ones. Islamic economics is based on the principle that Allah the Almighty created this world with plenty of resources that satisfy the needs of everyone. Thus one person's success is not necessarily achieved at the expense or exclusion of the success of others. This "win/win" framework leads to better economic behavior and performance, and thus promises better future for mankind. Islamic Banks are financial institutions established according to principles of Islamic Economics. They provide finance and financial services in a manner leading to mutual benefit. Although finance activities are deeply rooted in Islamic history, formal Islamic banking is a recent phenomenon, whereby the first Islamic bank was established around 1963.

C. The Islamic Finance system

One of the most important objectives of Islam is to realize greater justice in human society. According to the Qur'an all the messengers of God were sent to promote justice and any society where there is no justice will ultimately head towards decline and destruction. One of the essential requisites for ensuring justice is a set of rules or moral values, which everyone accepts and complies with faithfully. The financial system may be able to promote justice if, in addition to being strong and stable, it satisfies at least two conditions. One of these is that the financier should also share in the risk so as not to shift the entire burden of losses to the entrepreneur or the borrower, and the other is that an equitable share of the society's financial resources becomes available to even the poor on affordable terms in keeping with their ability to repay so as to enable them to realize their dream of owning their own homes, pursuing higher education and vocational training, and establishing their own micro enterprises.

To fulfill the first condition of justice, Islam requires both the financier and the entrepreneur to equitably share the profit as well as the loss. For this purpose, one of the basic principles of Islamic Finance is: "No risk, no gain."

This should help introduce greater discipline into the financial system by motivating financial institutions to assess the risks more carefully and to effectively monitor the use of funds by borrowers. The double assessment of risks by both the financier and the entrepreneur should help inject greater discipline into the system, and go a long way in not only increasing efficiency in the use of resources but also reducing excessive lending.

Islamic Finance is based on shariah, an Arabic term that is often translated into "Islamic law". Shariah provides guidelines for aspects of Muslim life, including religion, politics, economics, banking , business, and law. Shariah-compliant financing (SCF) constitutes financial practices that conform to Islamic law.

Islamic Finance was practiced predominantly in the Muslim world throughout the Middle Ages, fostering trade and business activities with the development of credit. In Spain and the Mediterranean and Baltic states, Islamic merchants became indispensable middlemen for trading activities. In fact, many concepts, techniques, and instruments of Islamic Finance were later adopted by European financiers and businessmen.

In contrast, the term "Islamic financial system" is relatively new, appearing only in the mid-1980s. In fact, all the earlier references to commercial or mercantile activities conforming to Islamic principles were made under the umbrella of either "interest free" or "Islamic" banking. However, describing the Islamic financial system simply as "interest-free" does not provide a true picture of the system as a whole. Undoubtedly, prohibiting the receipt and payment of interest is the nucleus of the system, but it is supported by other principles of Islamic doctrine advocating risk sharing, individuals' rights and duties, property rights, and the sanctity of contracts.

Similarly, the Islamic financial system is not limited to banking but covers capital formation, capital markets, and all types of financial intermediation. Interpreting the system as "interest free" tends to create confusion. The philosophical foundation of an Islamic financial system goes beyond the interaction of factors of production and economic behavior. Whereas the conventional financial system focuses primarily on the economic and financial aspects of transactions, the Islamic system places equal emphasis on the ethical, moral, social, and religious dimensions, to enhance equality and fairness for the good of society as a whole. The system can be fully appreciated only in the context of Islam's teachings on the work ethic, wealth distribution, social and economic justice, and the role of the state.

The Islamic financial system is founded on the absolute prohibition of the payment or receipt of any predetermined, guaranteed rate of return. This closes the door to the concept of interest and precludes the use of debt-based instruments. The system encourages risk- sharing, promotes entrepreneurship, discourages speculative behavior, and emphasizes the sanctity of contracts.

Modern Islamic Finance has existed internationally since the 1970s. Currently, Islamic Finance represents a small but growing segment of the global finance industry. In some countries, such as Iran and Pakistan, Islamic banks are the only mainstream financial institutions. In others, Shariah-compliant financing (SCF) exists alongside conventional banking. Estimates vary of the total size of assets held internationally under Islamic Finance, generally ranging from $800 billion to $1 trillion, with growth rates of 10% to 15% annually over the past ten years. The Persian Gulf and Southeast Asia historically have been and continue to be the major centers for SCF. For oil producers in the Gulf region, Islamic Finance may offer investment opportunities for their growing revenues from oil exports. There also has been a growing awareness of and demand for Islamic-based financial products by Muslim consumers. In 2007, Iran was the largest market for Islamic Finance, reportedly accounting for close to 40% of shariah-compliant financial assets worldwide.6 However, according to some analysts, the reach of Iran's Islamic Finance market may be limited because of international sanctions. Following Iran, the largest Islamic Finance markets in 2007 were Saudi Arabia, Malaysia, Kuwait, and the United Arab Emirates (UAE). Support for Islamic Finance varies in the Middle East. In some countries, such as Libya and Morocco, Islamic banks are considered by some to be tied to Islamic political parties and consequently have been refused licenses. Other countries, including Jordan, Tunisia, and the Sudan, have been receptive to Islamic Finance, viewing Islamic financial products as an opportunity for creating capital and fostering economic development.

In recent years, SCF has expanded to other parts of the world. Islamic Finance is growing in Europe and North

America, areas in which Muslims are in the minority. In August 2004, the United Kingdom's Financial Services Authority (FSA) approved a banking license for the Islamic Bank of Britain (IBB), the country's first Islamic bank. The IBB would serve the consumer market with shariah-compliant products. In March 2006, the FSA licensed the European Islamic Investment Bank as the United Kingdom's first independent bank for shariah-compliant investments.

In 1999, the Dow Jones presented its first Islamic market index, which follows shariah-compliant stocks internationally. The Dow Jones maintains more than 70 indices in its Islamic series and is advised by an independent Shariah Supervisory Board counsel.

1. Shari'a law defined

Shari'ah (or Islamic) law is meant to regulate all aspects of a Muslim's way of life. It is broadly divided into two sets of rules: one relates to the obligatory worship of God (ibadah) and the other relates to daily life outside the context of obligatory worship (muamalat), including commercial and financial dealings. Shari'ah is not a codified body of law. It consists of general rules and principles derived from the Qur'an (the Muslim holy book), the practices (sunnah) and sayings (ahadith) of the Prophet Mohammed (as discussed in further detail below). These general principles are capable of interpretation and development to address new issues or circumstances that arise from time to time.

Indeed, the Shari'ah has been supplemented by extensive Islamic jurisprudence (fiqh) developed over centuries by different schools of thought (the madhaa'hib). The key point to note is that, while all the schools of thought agree on the fundamental Shari'a principles enshrined in the Qur'an, sunnah and hadith, they sometimes hold differing views on their interpretation and application.

2. Sources of Shari'ah law

Shari'a law is derived from a number of primary and secondary sources.

a) Qur'an

The Qur'an is a primary source of law and is believed by Muslims to contain the word of God as revealed to the Prophet Mohammed. Evidence found in other sources of Shari'a law is subject to the Qur'an.

b) Sunnah

Sunnah literally means "well known path". The sunnah is a primary source of law and comprises traditional accounts of what the Prophet Mohammed said or did during his life which have legal content. Sunnah also comprises the sayings of others tacitly approved by the Prophet's silence.

c) Hadith

A further primary source of law is the narrative record of sayings and actions of the Prophet Mohammed known as hadith (plural ahadith). The extent to which sunnah is derived or differentiated from ahadith depends on the context and school of thought being considered.

d) Qiyas

Qiyas represents the process of reasoning whereby the principles found in the Qur'an and sunnah are extended to new cases by analogy.

e) Ijma

Ijma represents the consensus of the Islamic community (whether at a local or global academic level) on a particular issue.

(f) Ijtihad

Ijtihad is the interpretation and the opinion of Islamic jurists on a particular issue. Qiyas,ijma and ijtihad are all secondary sources of Shari'a law.

3. Issues relating to interpretation and application of Shari'a law Since Shari'a law is not a single codified body of law and is open to interpretation, the opinions of Shari'a scholars may differ on the same question of Shari'a law depending on the school of thought to which particular scholars belong. In addition, scholars' views on questions of Shari'a law may change over time. This can lead to uncertainty and inconsistency of interpretation and application of Shari'a law across the Islamic world.

4. key Shari'a Principles and Prohibitions Relevant to Finance

There are a number of key Shari'a principles and prohibitions relevant to finance and commercial transactions which distinguish Islamic Finance from the conventional forms. For completeness, it should be mentioned that there are two main branches within Islam: sunnism and shiaism. The majority of Muslims are sunni and the following is limited to the discussion of the general Shari'a principles relating to Islamic Finance within sunni jurisprudence. The key Shari'a principles which underpin Islamic Finance, and have led to the creation of a separate finance industry, are as follows:

a) Prohibition on usury and interest (riba)

Prohibition of interest. Prohibition of riba, a term literally meaning "an excess" and interpreted as "any unjustifiable increase of capital whether in loans or sales" is the central tenet of the system. More precisely, any positive, fixed, predetermined rate tied to the maturity and the amount of principal (i.e., guaranteed regardless of the performance of the investment) is considered riba and is prohibited. The general consensus among Islamic scholars is that riba covers not only usury but also the charging of "interest" as widely practiced.

This prohibition is based on arguments of social justice, equality, and property rights. Islam encourages the earning of profits but forbids the charging of interest because profits, determined ex post, symbolize successful entrepreneurship and creation of additional wealth whereas interest, determined ex ante, is a cost that is accrued irrespective of the outcome of business operations and may not create wealth if there are business losses. Social justice demands that borrowers and lenders share rewards as well as losses in an equitable fashion and that the process of wealth accumulation and distribution in the economy be fair and representative of true productivity.

Under the Shari'a, it is not permissible to charge, pay or receive interest. The Shari'a does not recognise the time value of money and it is therefore not permissible to make money by lending it. Money must be used to create real economic value and it is only permissible to earn a return from investing money in permissible commercial activities which involve the financier or investor taking some commercial risk. This prohibition is the main driving force behind the development of the modern Islamic Finance industry. Riba can take one of two forms: riba al-naseeyah and riba al-fadl.

1- Riba al-naseeyah is the amount of excess received by a lender in addition to the capital amount lent. This type of riba is comparable to the traditional concept of interest in conventional lending activities.

2- The second type, riba al-fadl, is excess compensation without any form of consideration in return.

In modern finance, riba al-fadl could be applicable to several exchange of commodities contracts.

The idea is that when compensation is paid, it should be justified or be set against a specific activity and the return should also be associated with a specific risk. Therefore when parties exchange commodities of similar value and one party pays excessive compensation to the other party, this is considered riba.

b) Prohibition on realising a gain from speculation (mayseer)

It is not permissible to earn a profit from speculation. Gambling is therefore not permitted under Shari'a. Any contracts or arrangements which involve speculation are also not permitted. That said,it is accepted under the

Shari'a that there is an element of speculation in most commercial arrangements and, unlike the absolute prohibition of interest, it is a question of the degree of speculation involved and whether the intention behind the transaction is to realise a gain from some productive effort or purely speculation.

The distinction between prohibited speculation and legitimate commercial speculation is not always clear in practice and there are examples where it can be difficult to distinguish between the two. For example, it is generally accepted that it is permissible to make an equity investment in a company engaging in a business activity that is permissible under the Shari'a with a view to realising future dividends and capital gains on the investment. There is of course a degree of commercial speculation involved about the future prospects of the company when an investor makes an equity investment, but whether such speculation is permissible or not would depend on the intention of the investor,i.e. was the intention to make a quick profit by speculating in the likely movement of the share price over a very short period of time (as is arguably the case with day trading), or was the decision made on the basis of careful evaluation of the company's past results and future prospects?

At the other end of the spectrum, equity derivatives such as index- linked derivatives are generally viewed as unacceptable under Shari'a because they involve speculation on the movement of an equity index.

c) No uncertainty (gharar) in commercial transactions

Certainty of terms in any transaction is a key requirement under the Shari'a. Again, as with speculation, a degree of commercial uncertainty is acceptable but there must not be any uncertainty about the key terms of the transaction. For example, in a transaction for the sale of assets, the sale contract should set out a clear description of the assets being sold, the sale price and the time for delivering the assets to the purchaser. Similarly, a leasing contract needs to set out clearly the assets which are being leased, the duration of the lease and the rent payable under the lease. One of the reasons that conventional insurance contracts are not considered permissible under the Shari'a is that there is no certainty as to when a claim will be paid, given that there is no way of knowing if and when the insured event will occur.

In the context of modern day Islamic Finance, key examples of gharar are:

(a) Advising a customer to buy shares of a particular company that is the subject of a takeover bid, on the grounds that its share price can be expected to rise;

(b) Buying a house, the price of which is to be specified in the future;

(c) When the subject matter or specifications to a contract are unknown; and

(d) Deferred payment under a contract where the deferment is for an unknown period.

d) All activity must be for permitted purposes (halal)

Muslims must not engage in (or derive any benefit from) activities which are prohibited under the Shari'a. It is therefore not permissible for Muslims to invest in businesses which engage in prohibited activities such as casinos, a breweries or a factories making pork products. It is also not permissible for Islamic banks to provide any financing to such businesses. However, a very strict interpretation of these rules would mean that Muslims would only be able to invest in a very limited number of businesses internationally. For example, it would not be permissible for Muslims to invest in a hotel that serve alcohol, a food company which also manufactures pork products as part of its product range or any business that lends or borrows money at interest.

In light of the practical considerations of international commerce and in order to enable Muslim investors to participate in it, a number of prominent Shari'a scholars have advanced the view that it is permissible for Muslims to invest in businesses or companies which are not entirely Shari'a compliant so long as certain conditions are met. These conditions include (among other things):

(a) The principal business activity must be permissible under

Shari'a;

(b) Any income derived from prohibited activities should only form a small percentage of the overall income of the company or business (this percentage ranges from 5 to 20 per cent. Of overall income depending upon the nature of the prohibited activity and the Shari'a scholars involved);

(c) The aggregate amount of interest-bearing debt incurred by a company or business must not exceed a certain percentage of its assets or market capitalisation (there are

disagreements
between Shari'a scholars as to what percentage is acceptable and it ranges from 25 to 35 per cent. of total assets or market capitalisation depending upon the scholars involved); and

(d) The accounts receivable of the company on the business must not exceed a certain percentage of its assets or market capitalisation (usually set between 25 and 33 per cent.).

e) Making Money from Money is not Permissible

One of the wrong presumptions on which all theories of interest are based is that money is a commodity. It is, therefore, argued that just as a merchant can sell his commodity for a higher price than his cost, he can also sell his money for a higher price than its face value, or just as he can lease his property and can charge a rent against it, he can also lend his money and can claim interest thereupon. Islamic principles, however, do not subscribe to this presumption. Money and commodity have different characteristics and, therefore, they are treated differently.

The basic points of difference between money and commodity:-

(a) Money has no intrinsic utility. It cannot be utilized in direct fulfillment of human needs. It can only be used for acquiring some goods or services. A commodity, on the other hand, has intrinsic utility and can be utilized directly without exchanging it for some other thing.

(b) Commodities can be of different qualities while money has no quality except that it is a measure of value or a medium of exchange. Therefore, all the units of money of the same denomination, are hundred per cent equal to each other. An old and dirty note of SR.100 has the same value as a brand

new note of SR.100.

(c) In commodities, the transactions of sale and purchase are effected on an identified particular commodity. If A has purchased a particular car by pinpointing it, and seller has agreed, he deserves to receive the same car. The seller cannot compel him to take the delivery of another car, though of the same type or quality. Money, on the contrary, cannot be pinpointed in a transaction of exchange. If A has purchased a commodity from B by showing him a particular note of 100 SR.100 he can still pay him another note of the same denomination.

Based on these basic differences, Islamic Shariah has treated money differently from commodities, especially on two scores: Firstly, money (of the same denomination) is not held to be the subject matter of trade, like other commodities. Its use has been restricted to its basic purpose i.e. to act as a medium of exchange and a measure of value. Secondly, if for exceptional reasons, money has to be exchanged for money or it is borrowed, the payment on both sides must be equal, so that it is not used for the purpose it is not meant for i.e. trade in money itself.

In short, money is treated as "potential" capital. It becomes actual capital only when it joins hands with other resources to undertake a productive activity. Islam recognizes the time value of money, but only when it acts as capital, not when it is "potential" capital.

5. Basic Islamic Financial Instruments

Islamic markets offer different instruments to satisfy providers and users of funds in a variety of ways: sales, trade financing, and investment. Basic instruments include cost-plus financing (murabaha), profit-sharing (mudaraba) ,leasing (ijara), partnership (musharaka) , and for ward sale (bay' salam), Deferred-payment sale (bay' mu'ajjal) and deferred-delivery sale (bay'salam) contracts, in addition to spot sales, are used for conducting credit sales. In a deferred-payment sale, delivery of the product is taken on the spot but delivery of the payment is delayed for an agreed period. Payment can be made in a lump sum or in installments, provided there is no extra charge for the delay. A deferred-delivery sale is similar to a forward contract where delivery of the product is in the future in exchange for payment on the spot market.

These instruments serve as the basic building blocks for developing a wide array of more complex financial instruments, suggesting that there is great potential for financial innovation and expansion in Islamic financial markets Some of the more popular instruments in Islamic financial markets are Trade with markup or cost-plus sale (murabaha).

One of the most widely used instruments for short-term financing is based on the traditional notion of purchase finance. The investor undertakes to supply specific goods or commodities, incorporating a mutually agreed contract for resale to the client and a mutually negotiated margin. Around 75 percent of Islamic financial transactions are cost-plus sales.

Murabaha was originally an exchange transaction in which a trader purchases items required by an end user. The trader then sells those items to the end-user at a price that is calculated using an agreed profit margin over the costs incurred by the trader.

To be in consonance with the principles of Islamic Finance governing exchange transactions every murabaha transaction must meet the following conditions:

Murabaha transactions may be undertaken only where the client of a bank, or financial institution, wants to purchase a commodity. This type of transaction cannot be effected in cases where the client wants to get funds for a purpose other than purchasing a commodity, like payment of salaries, settlement of bills or other liabilities.

To make it a valid transaction it is necessary that the commodity is really purchased by the bank and it comes into the ownership and possession (physical or constructive) of the bank so that it may assume the risk of the commodity so far as it remains under its ownership and possession.

After acquiring the ownership and possession of the commodity it should be sold to the client through a valid sale.

Some quarters have equated murabahah transactions to interest- based loans. However, there are many significant factors that distinguish a murabaha contract from a riba-based one. Some of them are the following:

In the event of default by the end user, the financer only has recourse to the items financed, and no further mark-up or penalty may be applied to the sum outstanding. This means that the amount to be repaid does not go on increasing with passage of time as in the case of amounts borrowed from conventional banks on interest.Also, in conventional financing, the bank gives loans to its clients without ever being concerned how the money is being put to use.

In the event of a murabahah transaction, no money is loaned to the client. Rather, the financing party purchases the goods himself, based on the requirement of the client. This ensures that financing is always asset-based. In effect, this type of financing creates real assets and inventories .

Another major difference between a murabahah contract and an interest-based one is that the financier cannot be unconcerned about the purposes for which the asset being leased is to be put to use. Conventional banks have no compunction in lending to gambling houses or liquor companies, or even pornographic filmmakers.

Islamic principles of finance are based on a well-established rule which dictates that "The benefit of a thing is a return for the liability for loss from that thing". Hence, in a murabahah transaction the bank or financier assumes the risk by purchasing the commodity before he sells it at a markup.

This mark up is considered as the reward of the risk he assumes. Interest-bearing loans assume no risks whatsoever. In other words, because the bank takes title to the goods, and is therefore engaged in buying and selling, its profit derives from a real service that entails a certain risk. This aspect lends the transaction legitimacy.

Most scholars have ruled that, to serve as a deterrent to such as may willfully delay payments, the financer may get the buyer to agree, at the time of the contract, to make a pre-specified donation to an agreed charity in case of late payment of monthly installments.

These scholars, however, caution that this device should be used to the minimum extent and only in cases where musharakah or mudarabah are not practicable for one reason or another.

B. Profit-sharing agreement (mudaraba). This is identical to an investment fund in which managers handle a pool of funds. The agent-manager has relatively limited liability while having sufficient incentives to perform. The capital is invested in broadly defined activities, and the terms of profit and risk sharing are customized for each investment. The maturity structure ranges from short to medium term and is more suitable for trade activities.

Mudaraba implies a contract between two parties whereby one party, the rabb al-mal (beneficial owner or the sleeping partner), entrusts money to the other party called the mudarib (managing trustee or the labour partner). The mudarib is to utilize it in an agreed manner and then returns to the rabb al-mal the principal and the pre-agreed share of the profit. He keeps for himself what remains of such profits.

The following rules must govern all Mudaraba transactions:

- The division of profits between the two parties must necessarily be on a proportional basis and cannot be a lump sum or guaranteed return.

- The investor is not liable for losses beyond the capital he has contributed. The mudarib does not share in the losses except for the loss of his time and efforts.

- Briefly, an Islamic bank lends money to a client to finance a factory, for example, in return for which the bank will get a specified percentage of the factory's net profits every year for a designated period. This share of the profits provides for repayment of the principal and a profit for the bank to pass on to its depositors. Should the factory lose money, the bank, its depositors and the borrower all jointly absorb the losses, thereby putting into practice the pivotal Islamic principle that the providers and users of capital should share risks and rewards.

Islamic banks use this instrument to finance those seeking investments to run their own enterprises or professional units, whether they be physicians or engineers or traders or craftsmen.

The bank provides the adequate finance as a capital

owner in exchange of a share in the profit to be agreed upon.

It is worth noting that this mode is a high risk for the bank because the bank delivers capital to the mudarib who undertakes the work and management and the mudarib shall only be a guarantor in case of negligence and trespass. Islamic banks usually take the necessary precautions to decrease the risk and to guarantee a better execution for the mudaraba and pursue this objective with seriousness.

However, it may be noted that, under mudarabah, the liability of the financier is limited to the extent of his contribution to the capital, and no more.

C. Equity participation (musharaka). This is analogous to a classical joint venture. Both entrepreneur and investor contribute to the capital (assets, technical and managerial expertise, working capital, etc.) of the operation in varying degrees and agree to share the returns (as well as the risks) in proportions agreed to in advance. Traditionally,this form of transaction has been used for financing fixed assets and working capital of medium- and long-term duration. Musharaka is a partnership, normally of limited duration, formed to carry out a specific project.

It is, therefore, similar to a Western-style joint venture, and is also regarded by some as the purest form of Islamic financial instrument, since it conforms to the underlying partnership principles of sharing in, and benefiting from, risk. Participation in a musharaka can either be in a new project, or by providing additional funds for an existing one. Profits are divided on a pre-determined basis, and any losses shared in proportion to the capital contribution. In this case, the bank enters into a partnership with a client in which both share the equity capital- and maybe even the management -of a project or deal, and both share in the profits or losses according to their equity shareholding. There are two basic types of musharaka:

i. Sharikah al milk: partnership based on joint ownership. This may be voluntary e.g. in the purchase of a ship, or involuntary e.g. as a result of inheritance.

ii. Sharikah al uqud: partnership based on a contractual relationship.

There are five subdivisions:

1. Sharikat al Mufawadah (full authority and obligation): a limited partnership with equal capital contributions, responsibility, full authority on behalf of others, and responsibility for liabilities,incurred through the normal course of business.

2. Sharikat al Inan (restricted authority and obligation): a limited partnership with unequal capital contributions. They do not share equal responsibility, and this reflects their share of the profits.

3. Sharikat al Wujuh (goodwill /credit worthiness): companies based on the reputation of one or both parties, typically small scale business.

4. Sharikat al Abdan (labour, skill and management): a company based on the contribution of human efforts, no capital contributions, again, typically small scale business.

5. Sharikat al Mudaraba: a mudaraba

D. Leasing (ijara). Another popular instrument, accounting for about 10 percent of Islamic financial transactions, is leasing. Leasing is designed for financing vehicles, machinery, equipment, and aircraft.

Different forms of leasing are permissible, including leases where a portion of the installment payment goes toward the final purchase (with the transfer of ownership to the lessee).

Ijarah can be defined as a process by which " usufruct of a particular property is transferred to another person in exchange for a rent claimed from him/her". In many respects, Ijarah resembles leasing as it is practiced in today's commercial world.

The distinguishing feature of this mode is that the assets remain the property of the Islamic bank to put them up for rent every time the lease period terminates so as not to remain unutilized for long periods of time. Under ijarah the bank or the leasing company assumes the risk of recession or diminishing demand for these assets.

To be in consonance with the principles of Islamic Finance governing financial transactions every ijarah transaction must meet the following conditions:

- It is a condition that the object leased must not be perishable or consumable.

- The lease is for the utilization not the consumption of the asset.

- It is a condition that the subject of the contract must actually and legally be attainable. It isnot permissible to lease something that cannot be delivered.

- The lessee must ensure that the asset is used for the purpose it is made for. The lessee shallcomply with the provisions of the contract. The lessee also shall not benefit from the asset in a way more than what has been agreed upon.

- It is not permitted to lease real estate to be used as an interest based bank or a bar. However it is permissible to lease property to those whose major activities are permissible or halal even if they include some secondary prohibited practices.

- The lessor must not only deliver the asset on time, on the date of commencement of lease, but also ensure that the lessor delivers those accessories as well which are essential for the lessee to benefit from the asset as per the norms.

- The lease contract must state the lease period clearly. Renewal terms must also be stated clearly, and things like the rentals for all subsequent years, after the first year, should not mention clauses like 'left to the sole discretion of the lessor' and the like.

- The rental must be money. The lease rent falls due from the receipt of the asset by the lessee,not the date the contract is signed.

- The amount and timing of the lease payments should be agreed in advance. However, theagreed schedule and amount of those payments need not be uniform.

- It is permissible for the two parties to agree during the lease period to review the lease period or the rental or both. That is because the lease contract occurs periodically unlike the sale contract where the transfer of ownership is immediate.

- The lessor bears the liabilities when leasing the asset such as damage to the asset, payment of premium cost and basic maintenance.

- There is no objection to authorizing the lessee to undertake all the above but the costs thereof must be borne by the lessor/owner.

- The lessor/owner bears all the costs of the legally binding basic maintenance and these are operations on which the permanence and suitability of the leased object depend. The lessor also bears the cost of the replacement of durable parts. However, it is permissible to make the lessee bear the cost of ordinary routine maintenance, because this cost is normally known and can be considered as part of the rental.

- The conditions of usage of the leased items must be stated. The lessor must have full possession and legal ownership of the asset prior to leasing it.

- A price cannot be pre-determined for the sale of the asset at the expiry of the lease. However,lessor and lessee may agree to the continuation of the lease or the sale of the leased asset to the lessee under a new agreement at the end of the initial lease period.

- In the event of late payment of rental, the Ijarah may be terminated immediately.
- The lessor may claim compensation for any damage caused to the leased assets as a result of negligence on the part of the lessee.

Literally, Ijarah means to give something on rent. As a term of Islamic Fiqh, Ijarah can also refer to wages paid to a person in consideration of the services rendered by him/her. In the above discussion, the term Ijarah is used to represent the usufructs of assets and properties, and not to the services of human beings.

E. Salam is one of the basic conditions for the validity of sale in Shariah that the commodity intended to be sold must be in the physical or constructive possession of the seller. This condition has three implications:

First, the commodity must be existing; a commodity that does not exist at the time of sale cannot be sold.

Second, the seller should have acquired the ownership of that commodity. If the commodity exists but the seller does not own it, he cannot sell it to anybody.

Third, mere ownership is not enough. It should have come in the possession of the seller, either physically or constructively. If the seller owns a commodity, but he has not acquired its delivery by himself or through an agent, he cannot sell it.

There are only two exceptions to this general principle in Shariah. One is Salam and the other is Istisna.

Both are sales of a special nature.

Salam, or Bay-Salaam as it is also called, is a sale whereby the seller undertakes to supply some specific goods to the buyer at a future date in exchange for an advanced price fully paid on the spot. Here the price is paid in cash, but the supply of the purchased goods is deferred. The buyer is called "Rabb-us-Salam", the seller is "Muslam ilaih", the cash price is "ra's-ul-mal", and the purchased commodity is termed as "muslam fih".

The Shariah allows Salam subject to certain conditions. The basic purpose of this sale was to meet the needs of the small farmers who needed money to grow their crops and to feed their family up to the time of their harvest. After the prohibition of riba they could not take usurious loans. Therefore, it was allowed for them to sell the agricultural products in advance.

Similarly, the traders of Arabia used to export goods to other places and to import other goods to their homeland. They needed money to undertake this type of business. They could not borrow from the usurers after the prohibition of riba. It was, therefore, allowed for them that they sell the goods in advance. After receiving their cash price, they could easily undertake the aforesaid business. Salam was beneficial to the seller, because he received the price in advance, and it was beneficial to the buyer also,because normally, the price in Salam used to be lower than price in spot sales.

The permissibility of Salam was an exception to the general rule that prohibits forward sales. Therefore,it was subjected to some strict conditions.

Conditions of Salam:

It is necessary for the validity of Salam that the buyer pays the price in full to the seller at the time of effecting the sale. This is necessary because in the absence of full payment by the buyer,it will be tantamount to a sale of debt against debt, which is expressly prohibited. Moreover, the basic wisdom behind the permissibility of Salam is to fulfill the instant needs of the seller. If the price is not paid to him in full, the basic purpose of the transaction will be defeated.

Salam can be effected in those commodities only whose quality and quantity can be specified exactly. The things whose quality or quantity is not determined by the specification cannot be sold through the contract of Salam. For example, the precious stones cannot be sold on the basis of Salam, because every piece of precious stones is normally different from the other either in its quality or in its size or weight and their exact specification is not generally possible.

Salam cannot be effected on a particular commodity or on a product of a particular field or farm.

For example, if the seller undertakes to supply wheat of a particular field, or the fruit of a particular tree, the Salam will not be valid, because there is a possibility that produce of that particular field or the fruit of that tree is destroyed before the delivery, and in the presence of this possibility the delivery remains uncertain. The same rule is applicable to every commodity whose supply is not certain. It is necessary that the quality of the commodity (intended to be purchased through Salam) be fully specified leaving no ambiguity that may lead to dispute. All the possible details in this respect must be expressly mentioned.

It is also necessary that the quantity of the commodity be agreed upon in unequivocal terms. If the commodity is quantified in weights according to the usage of its traders, its weight must be determined, and if it is quantified through measures, its exact measure should be known. What is normally weighed cannot be specified in measures and vice versa.

The exact date of delivery must be specified in the contract.

Salam cannot be effected in respect of those things that must be delivered at the spot. For example, if gold is purchased in exchange for silver, it is necessary, according to Shariah, that the delivery of both be simultaneous. Here, Salam cannot work. Similarly, if wheat is bartered for barley, the simultaneous delivery of both is necessary for the validity of sale, therefore, the contract of Salam in this case is not allowed.

It is permissible to draw a Salam sale contract on one whole thing but to be possessed at different times in specific parts.

Salam sale is not permissible on existing commodities because damage and deterioration cannot be assured before delivery on the due date. Delivery may become impossible.

Salam is permissible on a commodity of a specific locality if it is assured that it is almost always available in that locality and it rarely becomes unavailable.

The place of delivery must be stated in the contract if the commodity needs loading or transportation expenses.

It is permissible to take mortgage and guarantor on Salam debt to guarantee that the seller satisfies his obligation by delivering the commodity sold, which is a liability on the due date.

It is not permissible for the buyer of a Salam commodity to sell it before receiving it because that is similar to the prohibited sale of debts before holding. It is known that the Salam commodity is a liability debt on the seller and not an existing commodity. Instead of that, it is permissible for the buyer to draw a parallel Salam contract without connecting it to the first Salam contract.

Salam sale is suitable for the finance of agriculture operations, where the bank can transact with farmers who are expected to have the commodity in plenty during harvest either from their own crops or crops of others, which they can buy and deliver in case their crops fail. Thus the bank renders great services to the farmers in their way to achieve their production targets.

Salam sale is also used to finance commercial and industrial activities, especially phases prior to production and export of commodities and that is by purchasing them on Salam and marketing them for lucrative prices.

The Salam sale is applied by banks in financing craftsmen and small producers by supplying them with inputs of production as a Salam capital in exchange for some of their commodities to remarket.

The scope of Salam sale is large enough to cover the needs of various people such as farmers,industrialists, contractors or traders. It can cover the finance of operational costs and capital goods.

F. Istisna is the second kind of sale where a commodity is transacted before it comes into existence.

It means to order a manufacturer to manufacture a specific commodity for the purchaser. If the manufacturer undertakes to manufacture the goods for him, the transaction of Istisna comes into existence. But it is necessary for the validity of Istisna that the price is fixed with the consent of the parties and that necessary specification of the commodity (intended to be manufactured) is fully settled between them.

The contract of Istisna creates a moral obligation on the manufacturer to manufacture the goods, but before he starts the work, any one of the parties may cancel the contract after giving notice to the other.

But after the manufacturer has started the work, the contract cannot be cancelled unilaterally.

However, the party placing the order has the right to retract if the commodity does not conform to the specifications demanded.

Istisna as a Mode of Financing: can be used for providing the facility of financing in certain transactions,especially in the sector of house financing.

If the client has his own land and he seeks financing for the construction of a house, the financier may undertake to construct the house on that open land, on the basis of Istisna, and if the client has no land and he wants to purchase the land also, the financier may undertake to provide him a constructed house on the specified piece of land.

Since it is not necessary in Istisna that the price is paid in advance, nor is it necessary that it is paid at the time of the delivery, rather, it may be deferred to any time according to the agreement of the parties, therefore, the time of payment may be fixed in whatever manner they wish. The payment may also be in installments.

On the other hand, it is not necessary that the financier himself construct the house. He can enter into a parallel contract of Istisna with a third party, or may hire the services of a contractor (other than the client). In both cases, he can calculate his cost and fix the price of Istisna with his client in a manner that may give him a reasonable profit over his cost. The payment of installments by the client may start, in this case, right from the day when the contract of Istisna is signed by the parties, and may continue during the construction of the house and after it is handed over to the client. In order to secure the payments of installments, the bank, as a security, may keep the title deeds of the house or land, or any other property, until the client pays the last installment.

The bank, in this case, will be responsible for the construction of the house in full conformity with the specifications detailed in the agreement. In case of discrepancy, the financier will undertake such alterations at his own cost as may be necessary for bringing it in harmony with the terms of the contract.

The instrument of Istisna may also be used for project financing on similar lines. If a client wants to install machinery in his factory, and the machinery needs to be manufactured, the financier may undertake to prepare the machinery through the contract of Istisna according to the aforesaid procedure. The same principles will be fully applicable to the construction of a building for the industry.

Istisna contracts open wide fields of application for the Islamic banks to finance the public needs and the vital interests of the society to develop the Islamic economy. Istisna contracts are applied in high technology industries such as the aircraft industry, locomotive and ship building industries, in addition to the different types of machines produced in large factories or workshops. The Istisna contract is also applied in the construction industry for apartment buildings, hospitals, schools, and universities.

Difference between Istisna and Salam:

1. The subject of Istisna is always a thing that needs manufacturing, while Salam can be effected on anything, no matter whether it needs manufacturing or not.

2. It is necessary for Salam that the price is paid in advance, while it is not necessary in Istisna.

3. The contract of Salam, once effected, cannot be cancelled unilaterally, while the contract of Istisna can be cancelled before the manufacturer starts the work.

4. The time of delivery is an essential part of the sale in Salam while it is not necessary in Istisna that the time of the delivery be fixed.

5. The buyer may stipulate in the Istisna contract that the

commodity shall be manufactured or produced by a specific manufacturer, or manufactured from specific materials. This is not permitted in the case of Salam sale.

Difference Between Istisna and Ijarah :

It should also be kept in mind that the manufacturer, in Istisna, undertakes to make the required goods with his own material. Therefore, this transaction implies that the manufacturer shall obtain the material, if it is not already with him, and shall undertake the work required for making the ordered goods with it.

However, if the customer provides the material, and the manufacturer is required to use his labor and skill only, the transaction is not Istisna. In this case it will be a transaction of Ijarah whereby the services of a person are retained for a specified fee paid to him.

G. Islamic bonds (sukuk) and financial engineering Muslim jurists subject the buying and selling of debt obligations to certain conditions in order to comply with the prohibition of riba (interest), gharar (uncertainty), and maysir (gambling). specify these conditions in detail. In summary, the debt must be a genuine one i.e., it must not be a subterfuge to borrow money such as an asset-linked buy-back arrangement. The debtor must acknowledge the trade and creditors must be known, accessible, and sound. Trading must be on a spot basis and not against debt. Importantly, the price cannot be other than the face value. In line with these principles, early doctrine on interest-free finance disallowed corporate or government bonds and the discounting of bills. Pressures for innovation have resulted in finding a way out of these limitations, admitting 'financial engineering'. In particular, leasing-based bonds (sukuk al-ijara) have been developed. Although other sukuk have been issued, eg sukuk al-mudaraba, sukuk al-musharaka, sukuk al-murabaha, the ijara sukuk remains the most popular.

Sukuk means participation certificate, and is commonly referred to as an 'Islamic bond'. Techniques similar to conventional structured finance securities are employed, with sukuk akin to pass-through certificates. A sakk simply represents a proportional or undivided ownership interest in an asset or pool of assets . Islamic bonds are more useful if they can be traded on the secondary market to gain liquidity. As indicated above, certain requirements must be met with respect to the trading capacity of the bonds on the Islamic financial market. Specifically, they cannot represent a debt (in Islam, debt- selling is forbidden), as conventional bonds can. Instead they must constitute property of an approved asset. Such a bond is obtained through the securitization of the asset, the property of which is divided into equally valued units and incorporated in the sukuk certificates. The value of the sukuk thus remains connected to the value of the underlying asset. While they come in zero coupon and coupon versions, the productivity and return is linked to the profit of the underlying asset and not to an interest rate (although an interest rate such as LIBOR can be used as a 'benchmark').

Consider, for example, the case of the sukuk al-ijara. The originator holds assets (land, buildings, aircraft, ships, etc) that are to constitute the basis of the returns to the sukuk investor. These assets are sold by the originator to a special purpose vehicle (SPV) and then are leased back at a specified rental. The SPV securitizes the assets by issuing sukuk certificates that can be purchased by investors. Each sukukIn what ways does Islamic banking differ from conventional finance?

certificate represents a share in the ownership of the assets, entitling the investor to periodic distributions from the SPV funded by the originator's rental payments on the leased assets. The returns can be either fixed rate or floating rate (often referenced to LIBOR as a 'benchmark') depending on the originator.

So far, AAOIFI (the Accounting and Auditing Organization for Islamic Financial Institutions) has issued Standards for fourteen types of sukuk .These can be broadly grouped into sukuk that bear predetermined returns and sukuk that allow for sharing of profit and, in some instances, loss. Sukuk al-murabaha and sukuk al- murabaha are examples of profit-and-loss-sharing sukuk. To date, most issued sukuk have borne predetermined returns, and the majority of such sukuk have been sukuk al-ijara, frequently at a predetermined rate of return.

In fact, the basic structure of a sukuk is very flexible and can be varied in a number of ways. The underlying assets that are pooled and securitized can be ijara, murabaha, istisnaa or musharaka receivables, or combinations of them, and the rates of return can be fixed, floating or zero coupon. Investment risks (credit risk, interest rate risk, foreign exchange risk, market price risk, liquidity risk) are much the same as those of conventional bonds, and depend on the way the securitization is structured, although one unique risk is that of shari'a compliance, a factor which also governs the tradeability of the sukuk.

Indeed, it is the potential for tradeability that primarily makes for the popularity of sukuk al-ijara. Ijara, though less commonly employed than murabaha as an asset in Islamic banks' balance sheets offers much greater flexibility for the Islamic bond market. Each security called sukuk-al-ijara represents a pro rata ownership of physical assets as against a pro rata share in financial claims or debt in the case of sukuk-al-murabaha. While debt can only be transferred at par, ownership in physical assets can always be transferred at a mutually negotiated price. Hence sukuk-al-ijara allow for creation of a secondary market since they represent a share in the ownership of a physical asset.

Finally, Islam has laid down a number of conditions to ensure that credit expands in step with the growth of the real rector. Some of these conditions are:

1. The asset which is being sold or leased must be real, and not imaginary or notional;

2. The seller must own and possess the goods being sold or leased;

3. The transaction must be a genuine trade transaction with the full intention of giving and taking delivery; and

4. The debt cannot be sold and thus the risk of default associated with it must be borne by the lender himself.

The first condition will help eliminate most of the speculative and gambling transactions which involve notional goods and which constituted a major part of the derivatives transactions during the current crisis. The second condition will help ensure that the seller (or lessor) also shares a part of the risk to be able to get a share in the return. Once the seller (financier) acquires ownership and possession of the goods for sale or lease, he/she bears the risk. This condition will put a constraint on short sales, and thereby remove the possibility of a steep decline in asset prices during a downturn. The Shari'ah has, however, made an exception to this rule in the case of salam and istisna where the goods are not already available in the market and need to be produced or manufactured before delivery. This will help ensure that financing expands in step with the rise of the real economy and thereby help curb excessive credit expansion.

The third and the fourth conditions will not only help eliminate a great deal of speculative and derivatives transactions where there is no intention of giving or taking delivery, but also motivate the creditor to be more cautious in evaluating the credit risk. This will prevent an unnecessary explosion in the volume and value of transactions and also help keep the rise in debt to be in step with the rise of the real economy. It will also release a greater volume of financial resources for the real sector and, thereby, help expand employment and self-employment opportunities and the production of need-fulfilling goods and services.

The discipline that Islam wishes to introduce in the financial system may not materialize unless the governments reduce their borrowing from the central bank to a level that is in harmony with the goal of price and financial stability. Even borrowing from the private sector should be primarily for development that will increase its ability to repay. Borrowing for meeting current spending needs to be avoided except in extreme circumstances. This is because borrowing does not eliminate the ultimate need for sacrifice.

Without this consciousness about the ultimate need for sacrifice, the need for borrowing is most likely to become path dependent.

A number of objections may be raised here against these conditions. One of these is that hedging is a genuine need of the economy and the restrictions specified above may stand against it. Genuine hedging or insurance which is undertaken by a person or firm to provide protection against losses actually incurred has been recognized by Muslim jurists. However, what is prohibited is 'hedging' that is not related to a real transaction and is rather of a speculative and gambling nature. A second objection may be that all these conditions will tend to shrink the size of the economy by reducing the number and volume of derivatives transactions. There is not doubt that the number of transactions will be reduced. However, it will be primarily those transactions which are of a speculative and gambling nature and are generally recognized to be zero-sum games. These have rarely contributed significantly to total real output. The compounded annual rate of growth of total outstanding derivatives between 2000 and 2007 was 29.9 percent per annum while that in total real world output was only 3.1 percent per annum. Hence a decline in speculative and gambling transactions is not likely to hurt the real economy significantly. While a restriction on such transactions will cut the commissions earned by speculators during an artificially generated boom, it will help them avert losses and bankruptcy that become unavoidable during the decline and lead to a financial crisis.

6. ISLAMIC BANKING

THE EMERGENCE OF ISLAMIC BANKING in recent years is one of the most important trends in the economic sector, and with the estimated 1.6 billion Muslims worldwide, it's ripe for growth potential.

There has always been a demand among Muslims for financial products and services that conform to Shariah (Islamic Law). The development of viable alternatives to conventional finance increasingly enables Muslims to participate in the financial world without violating their Islamic principles and without bearing the economic penalty that comes from non-participation, especially with the recent growth of oil prices.

Currently, the Islamic banking industry consists of several hundred billion dollars, and more than 300 financial institutions in and outside the Muslim world. there is $300 billion in assets managed according to Islamic principles, ranging from commercial to investment banks and investment funds, all providing Islamic products.

Others estimate the industry to be even larger. Financial Services Authority, the financial services regulator in the United Kingdom, for example, recently suggested Islamic banking was as large as $500 billion. Standard & Poor's, a rating agency, estimates that the sukuk (deed) market has reached $70 billion, and will top the $160 billion mark by the end of the decade. Islamic financial services are now evolving from a niche market to the mainstream.

In addition to the sheer number of Muslims worldwide, global financial institutions are taking a strong interest in Islamic products since the industry is in its nascent stage. Products have yet to be commoditized from competition, therefore allowing profit margins to remain high.

What is Islamic banking?

Islamic banking can be considered banking with a conscience. Islamic banks each have a Shariah board made up of Shariah scholars as well as financial experts who are responsible for determining what activities are and are not Shariah-compliant.

Islamic banking is based on two main financial principles. Firstly, investment is to be made in the private sector through interest-free financing. Secondly, the development of financial instruments is to be done on the basis of profit and loss sharing as well as sharing risks.

Further, Islamic banking is built around Shariah, mainly prohibiting the charging of interest. Because Islam considers interest an unjustified increase of capital, with no effort made to earn it, it is considered of false value, and therefore is prohibited.

Howcvcr, there are many arguments about the prohibition of interest in Islam. The first argument is that interest rates have no moral foundation. The second is that abstinence from consumption is not a justification of rewards.

Lastly, some argue that there are risks to justify the supplement of payment for capital lending if the loan is guaranteed.

In addition to the prohibition of interest payments, Islamic law treats money strictly as a medium of exchange. In other words, money, in itself, does not have any inherent value, and therefore it should not lead to the production of more money. In Islamic banking, the creditor/debtor relationship is defined differently than in the secular financial world. The creditor, or provider, of funds who becomes a partner in a project assumes the risk activity with the entrepreneur and shares profits as well as losses.

The creation of incremental wealth justifies the share of profit between the borrower and the lender of money, but does not guarantee a fixed return.

Some of the principle instruments involved in the aforementioned form of resource mobilization include the following:

Trade financing and cost-plus mark-up on traded goods (murabaha).

Profit-sharing (mudarabah) and equity participation (musharaka) in which cost-sharing among partners is also included.

Rental on purchased equipment (ijara).

Islamic banking portfolio using secondary financing instruments, such as shares and stocks revolving around the above-mentioned instruments.

III. NATURE OF THE GLOBAL FINANCIAL AND ECONOMIC CRISIS

The world economy currently suffers from a global financial and economic crisis that has become severe since the second half of 2008. This global financial situation was triggered by the advent of the subprime mortgage crisis in the United States that became apparent from the mid-2007s.

The financial crisis began in July 2007 when a loss of confidence by investors in the value of securitized mortgages in the United States resulted in a liquidity crisis that prompted a substantial injection of capital into financial markets by the United States Federal Reserve, Bank of England and the European Central Bank. The difference between the interest rates on interbank loans and short-term U.S. government debt spread, an indicator of perceived credit risk in the general economy,spiked up in July 2007, remained volatile for a year, then spiked even higher in September 2008. In September 2008, the crisis deepened, as stock markets worldwide crashed and entered a period of high volatility, and a considerable number of banks, mortgage lenders and insurance companies failed in the following weeks.

The subprime mortgage crisis is the main reason for the current financial crisis and it is an ongoing financial crisis triggered by a dramatic rise in mortgage delinquencies and foreclosures in the United States, with major adverse consequences for banks and financial markets around the globe. The crisis, which has its roots in the closing years of the 20th century, became apparent in 2007 and has exposed pervasive weaknesses in financial industry regulation and the global financial system. Approximately 80% of U.S. mortgages issued in recent years to subprime borrowers were adjustable-rate mortgages. When U.S. house prices began to decline in 2006-07,refinancing became more difficult and as adjustable-rate mortgages began to reset at higher rates, mortgage delinquencies soared. Securities backed with subprime mortgages, widely held by financial firms, lost most of their value. The result has been a large decline in the capital of many banks and USA government sponsored enterprises, tightening credit around the world.

The financial crisis in the US housing market has evolved into a large-scale liquidity crisis as the banks, credit institutions and other players in the financial market preferred to hold cash rather than lending to each other amidst the rush to get rid of the so-called toxic assets. At the beginning, the companies affected were those directly involved in home construction and mortgage lending, and then came the financial institutions which had engaged in the securitization of mortgages. After the federal takeover of Fannie Mae and Freddie Mac on 7 September 2008, which at that point owned or guaranteed about half of the US's mortgage market. The 14th of September 2008 was the date when the financial crisis entered a severe-impact phase marked by failures of some prominent American and European banks, like the bankruptcy of Lehman Brothers, which is the largest in US history with Lehman holding $639 billion in assets.

The crisis has been deepening with a global reach since September 2008 affecting a wide range of financial and economic activities and institutions around the world. The early impacts of the current financial crisis have been ensued in various countries and industries in terms of overall tightening of credit, steep declines in financial markets, liquidity problems in equity funds, devaluation of the assets underpinning insurance contracts and pension funds, increased public debt due to provision of public funds to financial services and other affected industries, devaluation of some currencies and increased currency volatility. As a result, a considerable number of stock markets, banks, mortgage lenders and insurance companies worldwide collapsed.

As the crisis deepened, the governments of major developed and developing countries as well as international financial regulators attempted to take some mitigation actions and coordinate efforts to contain the crisis. These actions and efforts included substantial capital injection into financial markets and interest rate cuts by major central banks like the US Federal Reserve, Bank of England, and the European Central Bank. For example, the US, at the core of the crisis, enacted on 3 October 2008 the Emergency Economic Stabilization Act, creating a $700 billion Troubled Assets Relief Program to purchase failing bank assets, especially mortgage-backed securities, and inject capital into banks. The British government on 8 October 2008 also launched a £500 billion bailout plan which aimed at injecting capital into the financial system and nationalized most of the financial institutions in trouble. These stabilization attempts were followed by cuts in interest rates by central banks in the US (Fed), England, China, Canada, Sweden, Switzerland and the European Central Bank in a coordinated effort to aid world economy.

A. Structural Causes That Aggravated the Crisis (An Islamic perspective).

A number of Islamic economists believes that the global crisis was caused by the following:-

1. Large expansion in speculation transactions in financial markets, including those conducted through the Internet, until they overshadowed the real transactions, which are the very reason behind the establishment of financial markets. (They are intended to effect fluidity and facility in moving on from one investment to another). The nature of speculations makes them unproductive in the end, because they merely shift wealth from losers to winners.

2. The emergence of many transactions intended merely for speculations on prices. Ultimately, these transactions do not produce any added value in the market, yet huge amounts of money and great human capacities are invested in them.

3. The spread of the culture of quick profit ("if you can get away with it, then do it"), without any consideration of

the long-term results of transactions. Added to this is the deficiency of laws, regulations, and administrative instructions aimed at following up the new methods for creating new forms of transactions and contracts (and this is what the Enron Corporation did). One has to note that this culture also emanates from capitalism as an idea and philosophy. Hence, so long as the law cannot control people's behavior or get hold of them, why should they not appropriate maximum gains?

4. The shift of capitalism from the phases of service and production to the phase of financial capitalism and inflation of the financial sector's profits, which caused people to believe that this is the way to quick gaining of wealth. Thus, layers of mere financial transactions that incessantly move away from the real production sector accumulated and increased in size. This brought about the so-called theory of the upside-down pyramid — a pyramid which is characterized by instability.

5. The dependence on interest-based loans given as a basis in funding, a process which does not produce any added value by itself.

6. The prevalence of securitization, which gave rise to an easy spread of

7. the culture of "strike and place the burden on others." This is also due to the fact that financial institutions accepted securitization with few and undeveloped restrictions, when, on the other hand, there were newly developed methods designed to protect those who made the first strike.

7. Securitization also created interconnection among financial institutions.Consequently, all of these institutions fell with the fall of the first piece of domino.

8. The system of exchange and trade of debts, and expansion in the transactions of selling debts. Enormous investments were attracted to such transactions, which in fact do not result in any real increase in social production. In addition, they are often quickly influenced by the media and political events. This would not happen, if interest was not adopted as a system of finance and refinance.

9. Investors' natural trend of making financial investments directed towardexercising much caution. This led to an increase in the processes of derivatives. Which in turn , inflated the size of mere financial swaps and exchanges still further. Another consequence is the increased interconnection among institutions, something which accelerated the movement of the retrogressive impact from one institution to another.

10. Large dependence on public debt rather than taxes. This generated inflation in the processes of financial exchanges, local and international.

11. Big rise in the US military spending.

12. Although it increases labor and employment, it does not tend to improve the productive capacity of the economy. In consequence, the competitive capacity of US products in foreign markets diminished and the deficit in the balance of trade accumulated, thus undermining confidence in the US economy.

B. Impact of The Global Crisis .

The global economy is now undergoing a deep economic downturn, with negative effects on both financial and real sectors not only in developed countries but also in developing countries. Most of the developing countries which survived the first wave of the storm due to little or no exposure to subprime mortgages are now being severely affected. Indeed, developing countries are now exposed to the global crisis more than in the previous occurrences given that they are currently more integrated with the global economy through trade, FDI, and remittances. Therefore, the current crisis, though rooted and deepened in developed countries, is now imposing serious adverse effects on developing countries, particularly those with high level of integration in world economy and international markets. In this context, the main transmission channels have been through the contraction of international trade and accompanying fall in commodity prices and the reversal of financial flows. Consequently, the following problems have been the major gifts of the crisis to developing countries:

1. Slowdown in economic growth It is commonly believed that the forthcoming recession in the world economy due to the crisis will be the worst since the Great Depression of 1930s, with negative world economic growth for 2009, particularly for the major developed countries like the US, Canada, the UK and Japan as well as the Euro area. Moreover, world economic outlooks of many international developmental agencies and institutions are still revised downwards. For example, while, in October 2008,

the IMF predicted a worldwide growth for 2009 by 3.0%, this was later revised down twice to 2.2% and then to 0.5%. Lastly, the WEO Report of April 2009 announced a projection of further contraction by 1.3% in world output in 2009 with leading advanced economies to experience a sharp contraction in growth while the developing countries to have a growth rate as low as 1.6%.

IMF's April World Economic Outlook has revealed that the slowdown in global economic activity will continue in 2009 while 2010 will mark a sluggish recovery. global economic growth will decrease from 3.2 percent in 2008 to -1.3 percent in 2009.

Similarly, in developing and emerging economies, growth will show a sharp decline from 6.1 percent in 2008 to 1.6 percent in 2009. In the Ole member countries, on average, output growth will decline significantly from 5.1 percent in 2008 to 1.5 percent in 2009.

2. Fall in export demand and commodity prices

WTO estimates show that the volume of global exports in goods and services will decrease by 9% in 2009, the largest decline since World War II. Exports will fall by 10% in developed countries while in developing countries exports will fall by 2-3% in 2009. Given the fact that most of the developing countries like China, India, Turkey, Korea, Malaysia, and many others rely heavily on trade to attract investment, createc jobs, and reduce poverty, the fall in exports will pose severe socio- economic implications for these economies.

Another blow to exports earnings of developing countries will come from decreasing commodity prices. The

World Bank estimates that energy prices will decline by 25% while non- energy commodity prices will decline by 23% in 2009. Another related problem will be looming in the area of trade financing. Global trade is highly dependent on trade credit and nearly 90% of trade is traditionally financed by the short term credit. Now, due to financial and economic crisis the credit market has been dried up. In 2008, WTO estimated a trade financing gap of US$ 25 billion which will further aggravate prospects for the developing countries which are more dependent on trade.

3. Sharp drops in private capital inflows

Foreign Direct Investment (FDI) is considered as a major source of financing for both public and private sectors in the developing countries lacking strong domestic financial systems. Amid the current financial and economic crisis, global FDI flow has shown downward trend and, according to UNCTAD, global FDI fell by 21 percent annually in 2008, after five years of strong growth and a record level of US$1.8 trillion in 2007. Developed countries witnessed the sharpest downturn of 33 percent while FDI flows to developing countries remained positive in 2008. However, growth rate decreased from over 20 percent in 2007 to 3.6 percent in 2008. Developing countries in regions like Africa which received huge amount of FDI in recent years may face sharper decline in FDI mainly triggered by the decrease in commodity prices, as most of the FDI in these economies was resource motivated.

4. Interruption in flows of ODA and remittances

Official Development Assistance (ODA) has been an important source of financing for many developing countries. UNCTAD publication has shown that banking crisis in donor countries during the past 30 year confirm a positive correlation between banking crisis and shrinking ODA. Provided the fact that developed countries were falling short of their commitments even before the onset of current financial and economic crisis, UNCTAD expects that crisis will cast negative impacts on flow of ODA to low income developing countries, thus further aggravating the prospects for achieving the Millennium Development Goals (MDGs) in these countries. In this regard, OIC member countries, especially those classified among the least developed countries will be hard hit by decrease in ODA flow. Over the years remittances has also emerged as an important source of finance for the developing countries. In 2008, developing countries received US$ 305 billion inflow of remittances. However, due to financial crisis, growth rate of inflow decreased from 22% in 2007 to 8% in 2008. Provided the fact that financial crisis has severely damaged the developed economies where majority of workers from developing countries are employed; remittances inflow to developing countries is expected to fall by 5 to 8 percent in 2009. Although remittances inflow will show negative growth across all developing regions, some regions like South Asia (SA) and Europe & Central Asia (ECA) will witness sharpcr dccline compared to other regions .

5. High exchange-rate volatility

The current crisis has led to higher exchange rate volatility that translates into increasing uncertainty and rising costs of international trade. Until the summer of 2008, the US dollar had weakened against the euro, but in the afterwards and especially after the collapse of Lehman Brothers in mid- September, the US dollar appreciated against the euro as well as British pound (GBP). The increasing risk aversion worldwide that results in a significant increase in portfolio flows into the US in addition to a widespread shortage of dollar liquidity in financial markets contributed to the appreciation of the dollar.

In this regard, most of the currencies of the developing countries including those with a pegged exchange rate to the euro have depreciated against the dollar. On the other hand, those with a pegged rate to the dollar have experienced appreciation in their currencies. To the extent that the changes in nominal exchange rates turn into movements in real exchange rates.

6. Deterioration in current account balances

The decline in global demand, the fall in commodity prices, and the credit crunch in the export markets have been the main sources of the decrease in the volume of exports worldwide. Therefore, countries are already facing or will soon be facing declines in export revenues, indicating a clear shock

on current account balances, although some countries also have lower import values due to lower commodity and oil prices. On the other hand, the decline in remittances inflows is also an important element of the negative impact of the crisis on the current account balances of many developing countries. In light of the recent estimates by the IMF, the advanced economies will have a slight improvement in their current account deficit in 2009 while the emerging and developing countries see a sharp decline in their surplus. Africa and the Middle East will suffer deficits unlike the developing Asian countries, which will experience an increase in their surplus. On the other hand, the OIC member countries, which have been giving increasing surpluses in recent years (above $400 billion in 2008), will face a deficit of around $35 billion, due mainly to sharp decline in oil revenues of the major oil exporting countries in the Middle East.

7. Increase in unemployment

The global economic slowdown triggered by the crisis is leading to a rapid rise in nemployment.

New investment/business projects are being postponed and most of the current ones are on hold due to the negative effects on the real economy and the pessimistic perceptions caused by the crisis. Given the slowdown in economic activity and the decrease in the volume of production as a result of the weak global demand, the business sector has had to reduce workforce to save cost. Consequently, many developed countries, in particular the US, are experiencing substantial increases in unemployment. Unemployment rate in the US has been significantly rising in recent months, reaching up to

8.5 percent in March 2009 compared to 6.2 percent in September 2008. Since the beginning of the recession in December 2007, 5.1 million jobs have been lost, with almost two-thirds (3.3 million) of the decrease occurring in the last 5 months At the other side, developing countries are also suffering unemployment pressures imposed by the crisis. Before the current crisis, many low- and middle-income countries were severely affected by increases in food and fuel prices while some others obtained significant gains. Now, with a fall in global demand, prices have fallen, to the advantage of net importers but to the detriment of those more dependent on export revenues, with rising unemployment pressures in the export sectors.

According to the ILO, due to the crisis, at least 20 million jobs will have been lost globally by the end of 2009. These jobs, which are predicted to be mostly in construction, real estate, financial services and auto sectors, will bring world unemployment above 200 million for the first time.

C. Views on the Solutions

It is widely agreed that the downside risks to the world economic growth calls for concerted and coordinated policy action at national and international level. As IMF described it, the current crisis is partly a "crisis of confidence", confidence in the global financial system. Restoring confidence in international financial system is key to resolving the crisis, and thus, greater international policy cooperation is crucial. The current global crisis and economic conditions could rebound faster than anticipated if policy measures at both national and international levels are credibly strengthened.

Recommendations by the Commission of Experts on Reforms of the International Monetary and Financial System Led by Nobel Laureate Joseph Stiglitz and commissioned by the President of the General Assembly, a group of experts proposed far-reaching changes in the international financial structure, and strong measures to overcome the current global economic crisis. The recommendations focused on the following titles:

1. All developed countries should take strong, coordinated, and effective actions to stimulate their economies.

Stimulus should be timely, have large "multipliers," help address the strains posed by the economic downturn on the poor, help address long run problems and prevent instability. While the decision on stimulus is national, it should be judged on its global impacts; if each country looks only at the national benefits versus costs, e.g. an increased national debt, the size of the global stimulus will be too small, spending will be distorted, and the global impact will be eviscerated. National stimulus packages should thus include spending measures to be undertaken in developing countries to offset the impact of the decline in world trade and financial market disintermediation. Industrialised countries should thus dedicate 1.0 per cent of their stimulus packages, in addition to traditional official development assistance commitments.

2. Developing countries need additional funding.

More permanent and stable sources of funding for developing countries that could be activated quickly and are not subject to inappropriate conditionality are necessary. Indeed, additional funding would be required just to offset the imbalances and inequities created by the massive stimulus and bail-out measures introduced in advanced industrialized countries. Such funding could be provided by an issuance of Special Drawing Rights approved by the IMF

Board in September 1997 through the proposed Fourth Amendment of the Articles of Agreement to double cumulative SDR allocations to SDR 42.8 billion and through the issuance of additional SDRs through standard procedures.

In addition regional efforts to augment liquidity should be supported. For instance, extension of liquidity support under the Chiang Mai initiative without an IMF program requirement should be given immediate consideration. Regional cooperation arrangements can be particularly effective because of a greater recognition of cross border externalities and greater sensitivities to the distinctive conditions in neighboring countries.

These additional sources of funding should be in addition to traditional official development assistance. Failure to maintain the levels of official assistance will have long-term effects. There will be an increase in poverty and malnutrition and the education of many young people will be interrupted, with life-long effects. The sense of global social solidarity will be impaired, making agreement on key global issues, such as responding to the challenges of climate change, more difficult. Failure to provide such assistance can be counterproductive even in a more narrow sense: it can impair the global recovery.

Developed countries must make a renewed effort to meet the commitments made in the Millennium Declaration, the Monterrey Consensus, the 2005 Global Summit, and the Doha Declaration by 2015.

3. Mobilizing Additional Development Funds by the Creation of a New Credit Facility.

The creation of a new credit facility is thus a matter of urgency. If such a facility could be created in a timely way, it could be a major vehicle for the disbursement of the requisite additional funding.

Given the need for rapid response, the new credit facility might be more quickly established under the umbrella of existing institutions, such as the World Bank, where efforts are underway to remedy existing inadequacies in governance and lending practices, or in Regional Development Banks where developing countries have more equitable representation. Or alternative institutional arrangements that create competition amongst institutions providing financial assistance might be envisaged. Such competition might not only increase the efficiency of disbursement, but also reduce the application of procyclical conditionality linked to financial support.

Whatever form is chosen, the new facility should have governance more reflective of democratic principles, with strong representation of developing countries and those countries contributing to the facility. These new governance arrangements might provide lessons for the reform of existing institutions.

Administration of the Facility could be done by staff seconded from existing multilateral financial institutions or central banks. The new facility could draw upon financial contributions from all countries. It could leverage any equity funds contributed by borrowing, including on the market or from those with large reserves or Sovereign Wealth Funds. Its ability to borrow could be enhanced through guarantees provided by governments, especially those of the advanced industrial countries. These alternative arrangements should be seen as a complement to expanded financial support from existing institutions,

4. Developing Countries need more policy space

There are asymmetries in global economic policies—countercyclical policies are pursued by developed countries, while most developing countries are encouraged or induced to pursue pro-cyclical policies. While this is partly due to the lack of resources to pursue countercyclical policies, it is also due to misguided policy recommendations from international financial institutions.

Conditionality attached to official lending and support for international financial institutions has often required developing countries to adopt the kinds of monetary and regulatory policies which contributed to the current crisis. In addition, these conditional ties contribute to global asymmetries, disadvantage developing countries relative to the developed, and undermine incentives for developing countries to seek support funding, contributing to global economic weakness. While the IMF initiatives to reduce conditional ties are to be commended, they might be insufficient, while in many cases countries are still required to introduce pro-cyclical policies.

5. The lack of coherence between policies governing trade and finance must be rectified.

Policy space is circumscribed not only by a lack of resources, but also by international agreements and by the conditional ties that often accompany assistance. Many bilateral and multilateral trade agreements contain commitments that circumscribe the ability of countries to respond to the current crisis with appropriate regulatory, structural, and macro-economic reforms and rescue packages, and may have exposed them unnecessarily to the contagion from the failures elsewhere in the global economic system. Developing countries especially need policy frameworks that can help protect them from regulatory and macro-economic failures in systemically significant countries. Developing countries have had imposed on them not only deregulation policies akin to those that are now recognized as having played a role in the onset of the crisis, but also have faced restrictions on their ability to manage their capital account and financial systems (e.g. as a result of financial and capital market liberalization policies); these policies are now exacting a heavy toll on many developing countries.

6. Crisis response must avoid protectionism Overt protectionism includes tariffs and domestic restrictions on procurement contained in some stimulus packages. Because of complex provisions and coverage of international trade agreements, seemingly "symmetric" provisions (e.g. exceptions of the application of provisions to countries covered by particular WTO or other international agreements) can have markedly asymmetric effects. Subsidies, implicit and explicit, can, as has been noted, be just as distorting to open and fair trade. There may, in some cases, be pressure for banks receiving large amounts of government assistance to focus on lending domestically. While the temptation that gives rise to such measures is under-

standable, efforts need to be made to finance additional support to developing countries to mitigate the impact of the crisis as well as of both open and hidden subsidies (i.e. state assistance through lending programs and guarantees) in order to avoid further distortions.

7. Opening advanced country markets to least developed countries' exports.

While a successful completion of the Doha trade round would be welcome, its impact on the crisis and its development dimension are still unclear .There are, however, a number of measures that have already been agreed in multilateral trade negotiations which could be implemented rapidly to support developing countries impacted by the crisis. These include implementation of duty free, quota-free market access for products originated from LDCs. In addition, the agreement reached at the WTO´s Hong Kong Ministerial session in 2005 provided for the elimination of all forms of developed country export subsidies, at the latest by 2013, should be implemented immediately. There is no reason to await a general agreement before implementing these measures. In addition, domestic support for cotton subsidies should be abolished immediately, as they distort prices to the detriment for African countries. More generally, in all trade negotiations, the long recognized principle of special and differential treatment of developing countries should be preserved.

8. Learning from Successful Policies to undertake Regulatory Reforms.

The financial crisis is widely viewed to be the result of the failure of regulatory policies in the advanced industrial countries. While full regulatory reforms will take time, it is imperative that work on regulatory reform begin now. The collapse in confidence in the financial system is widely recognized as central in the economic crisis; restoration of confidence will be central in the recovery. But it will be hard to restore confidence without changing the incentives and constraints facing the financial sector. It is imperative that the regulatory reforms be real and substantive, and go beyond the financial sector to address underlying problems in corporate governance and competition policy, and in tax structures, giving preferential treatment to capital gains, that may provide incentives for excessive leverage. While greater transparency is important, much more is needed than improving the clarity of financial instruments. Even if there had been full disclosure of derivative positions, their complexity was so great as to make an evaluation of the balance sheet position of the financial institutions extraordinarily difficult. Still, there is need for much greater transparency, including forbidding off balance sheet transactions and full expensing of employee stock options.

Well regulated economies have to be protected from competition from economies with inadequate or inappropriate regulatory systems. The problems of regulatory arbitrage and tax evasion are closely linked. Tax havens and financial centers in both developed and developing countries that fail to meet basic standards of transparency, information exchange and regulation should be given strong incentives to reform their practices, e.g. by restricting transactions between financial institutions in those jurisdictions and those in more highly regulated countries. Institutional arrangements for improving harmonization and transparency should be strengthened, including the United Nations Committee of Experts on International Cooperation in Tax Matters as proposed in Paragraph 16 of the Doha Declaration. Also other international arrangements and conventions such as United Nations Convention against Corruption should also be strengthened.

9. Coordinating the Domestic and Global Impact of Government Financial Sector Support Government bail-outs have substantial redistributive consequences that must be analysed in assessing their impact on recovery. In addition, because of the urgency of the situation they often fail to observe principles of good governance and especially of democratic transparency. This may lead to the introduction of inappropriate incentives, as well as failure to recognise possible adverse effects on other countries, especially on developing countries that lack equivalent financial resources.

Developed countries should undertake their financial support policies recognising that even symmetric policies can have asymmetric effects because guarantees by developing country governments are likely to be less meaningful than those by developed countries.

Failure to recognise these wider domestic and global consequences of financial support measures have often meant that the costs to the government and to developing countries have been higher than necessary. Funds have often been redistributed to those with higher incomes, and have created distorted incentives.

Support measures for financial institutions that are implemented by Central Banks risk imposing high costs on the public purse, without adequate parliamentary oversight of appropriations. Greater transparency on the part of all parties would facilitate a more effective response to the crisis.

10. Improved coordination of global economic policies

There is a need for substantial improvement in the coordination of global economic policy. Global economic integration has outpaced the development of the appropriate political institutions and arrangements for governance of the global economic system.

Remedying this lacuna is a matter of urgency, but this will not happen overnight. In the short term, there should be an appropriate mechanism within the United Nations System for independent international analysis on questions of global economic policy, including its social and environmental dimensions. Following the successful example of the Intergovernmental Panel on Climate Change (IPCC), a similar panel could be created to offer consultancy to the General Assembly and ECOSOC, but also to other international organizations to enhance their capacity for sound decision-making in these areas. At the same time, such a panel would contribute to foster a constructive dialogue and offer a regular venue for fruitful exchange between policy makers, the academic world and key international organizations. The panel should comprise well respected academics from all over the world, appropriately representing all continents, as well as representatives of international social movements. Being made up of outstanding specialists, the panel should be able to follow, analyze and assess long-term trends, key developments and major dynamics for global change affecting all people around the globe, identify problems in the global economic and financial architecture, and jointly provide options for coherent international action and recommendations for political decision making processes.

D. An agenda for systemic reform

The report of the experts also included an "agenda for systemic reform" to the international system that suggested;

1. A New Global Reserve System

The global imbalances which played an important role in this crisis can only be addressed if there is a better way of dealing with international economic risks facing countries than the current system of accumulating international reserves. Indeed, the magnitude of this crisis and the inadequacy of international responses may motivate even further accumulations. Inappropriate responses by some international economic institutions in previous economic crises have contributed to the problem, making reforms of the kind described here all the more essential. To resolve this problem a new Global Reserve System—what may be viewed as a greatly expanded SDR, with regular or cyclically adjusted emissions calibrated to the size of reserve accumulations—could contribute to global stability, economic strength, and global equity. Currently, poor countries are lending to the rich reserve countries at low interest rates. The dangers of a single-country reserve system have long been recognized, as the accumulation of debt undermines confidence and stability. But a two (or three) country reserve system, to which the world seems to be moving, may be

equally unstable. The new Global Reserve System is feasible, non- inflationary, and could be easily implemented, including in ways which mitigate the difficulties caused by asymmetric adjustment between surplus and deficit countries.

2. Reforms of the Governance of the International Financial Institutions

There is a growing international consensus in support of reform of the governance, accountability, and transparency in the Bretton Woods Institutions and other no representative institutions that have come to play a role in the global financial system, such as the Bank for International Settlements, its various Committees, and the Financial Stability Forum. These deficiencies have impaired the ability of these institutions to take adequate actions to prevent and respond to the crisis, and have meant that some of the policies and standards that they have adopted or recommended disadvantage developing countries and emerging market economies. Major reforms in the governance of these institutions, including those giving greater voice to developing countries and greater transparency are thus necessary. The reform of the World Bank's governance structure should be completed swiftly.

For the second stage of the reform, focussing on the realignment of shares, three criteria could be taken into account: economic weight, contribution to the development mandate of the World Bank (for example, measured in terms of contributions to IDA and trust funds), and the volume of borrowing from the Bank. For the IMF, serious consideration should be given to restoration of the weight of basic votes and the introduction of double or multiple majority voting. Elections of the leaders of the World Bank and the International Monetary Fund should take place under an open democratic process.

3. A Global Economic Coordination Council.

A globally representative forum to address areas of concern in the functioning of the global economic system in a comprehensive way must be created. At a level equivalent with the General Assembly and the Security Council, such a Global Economic Council should meet annually at the Heads of State and Government level to assess developments and provide leadership in economic, social and ecologic issues. It would promote development, secure consistency and coherence in the policy goals of the major international organizations and support consensus building among governments on efficient and effective solutions for issues of global economic, governance. Such a Council could also promote accountability of all international economic organizations, identify gaps that need to be filled to ensure the efficient operation of the global economic and financial system, and help set the agenda for global economic and financial reforms. It would be supported intellectually by the work of the International Panel discussed in III.10. Representation would be based on the constituency system, and designed to ensure that all continents and all major economies are represented. At the same time, its size should be guided by the fact that the council must remain small enough for effective discussion and decision making All important global institutions, such as the World Bank, IMF, WTO, ILO and members of the UN Secretariat dealing with economic and social issues would provide supporting information and participate in the Council. It could thus provide a democratically representative alternative to the G-20.

4. Better and more balanced surveillance.

The surveillance of economic policies should be especially focused on systemically significant countries, those whose bad performance is most likely to have global consequences. Such surveillance should focus not just on inflation, but on unemployment, financial stability, systemic stability related to the presence of built in stabilizers or destabilizers, and systems of social protection.

5. Reforming Central Bank Policies to promote Development Whereas price stability is desirable in support of growth and financial stability, it is not sufficient. Central Banks should therefore aim to ensure price stability in the context of delivering long-term sustainable growth, while being sensitive to the risks to financial stability, capital flows and exchange rates. Central banks also need to give consideration to financial market and asset price developments. This may entail Central Banks using a wider range of instruments, including prudential instruments.

A distinction may need to be made between the roles of

Central Banks in maintaining financial stability under normal circumstances and during crisis periods. Central Bank governance arrangements may need to differ depending on their precise role. In particular, in any actions which may impose serious risks on a country's fiscal position, such as those now being implemented in many countries as part of financial institution resolutions, should be subject to coordination.

6. Financial Market Policies

Financial policies, including regulation, have as their objective not only ensuring the safety and soundness of financial institutions and stability of the financial system, but protection of bank depositors, consumers and investors and ensuring financial inclusion - such as access to all banking services including credit, and the provision of financial products which help individuals and families manage the risks they face and gain access to credit at reasonable terms. It is also imperative to make sure that the sector is competitive and innovative. Financial institutions have been allowed to grow to be too big to fail, imposing enormous risk on the global economy. And while there has been innovation, too much of the innovation was aimed at regulatory, tax, and accounting arbitrage, and too little at meeting the real needs of ordinary citizens. Too little was done to help developing countries and ordinary homeowners manage the risks which they face, with consequences that have been repeatedly apparent. Financial regulation must be designed so as to enhance meaningful innovation that improves risk management and capital allocation. The current crisis has made it apparent that there are large gaps and deficiencies in the regulatory structures in place in many systemically significant countries. It is also apparent that while effective regulatory system must be national there must be some global regulatory framework to establish minimum national standards and also govern the global operations of systemical relevant global financial institutions. The Report of the Commission will identify a number of key aspects of regulatory reform, emphasizing the need for deep and pervasive reforms and highlighting the risks of merely cosmetic changes in regulations. The following items are among the key aspects of needed reform.

(a) Financial Product Safety

Sustainable recovery will depend on appropriate regulations (across countries, products, and institutions). Regulations should be based on what things are, not what they are called, i.e. insurance products should be regulated the same way, whether called insurance or not. Financial regulators should be mandated to ascertain the safety and appropriate use of various financial instruments and practices, including through the creation of a Financial Products Safety Commission.

Core depository institutions should be restricted from undertaking excessively risky activities and tightly regulated. There also needs to be close oversight over all highly levered and all systemically significant institutions. But there should be oversight over all financial institutions. Institutions can quickly change into systemically significant.

(b) Comprehensive Application of Financial Regulation

The fact that correlated behavior of a large number of institutions, each of which is not systemically significant, can give rise to systemic vulnerability makes oversight of all institutions necessary. There needs to be tighter regulation of incentives, especially in the core institutions; part of the current problem is a result of distorted incentives which encouraged short sighted and excessively risky behavior. It may be easier to regulate incentives than every manifestation of perverse incentives. There need to be restrictions on leverage, with automatic countercyclical capital adequacy and/or provisioning requirements.

Although the activities of private investment funds, equity funds and hedge funds did not trigger the financial crisis, their regulation is not globally uniform, creating the potential for regulatory arbitrage and the potential for gaps in regulation. Funds should be registered in the countries of their operations and provide appropriate regulation to regulatory authorities. In addition, banks must define limits for transactions with hedge funds.

There should be no retreat from mark to market accounting for institutions with short term funding in order to provide full transparency for investors and regulators. Other institutions may be encouraged to supplement mark-to-market accounting with valuations that are more appropriate to the maturity of their liabilities. In addition, steps should be taken to enforce transparency norms and public accountability for all public companies.

(c) Regulation of derivatives trading

The large scale use of unregulated, unsupervised OTC

derivatives has resulted in undue complexity, opacity, and mis-pricing of these instruments, and facilitated capital avoidance by financial institutions. These practices have weakened our financial system significantly and made resolution of failing firms extremely difficult.

Where appropriate steps should be take to develop regulated exchanges for trading standardized contracts of systemically significant derivative contracts, with the associated regulatory restrictions including limits on non-commercial traders.

Regulations should insure that derivative instruments are held on balance sheets, valued at independently audited real transaction prices, with appropriate capital provisioning, and clarity of purpose. The use of over the counter contracts by core institutions should, in general, be discouraged, but whenever used, there should be ample and adequate margin.

(d) Regulation of Credit Rating Agencies

Other needed reforms, including for Credit Rating Agencies and systems of information provision are addressed in an Appendix.

(e) Towards global institutional arrangements for governing the global economy.

The Financial Stability Forum was created in the aftermath of the 1997-8 financial crisis in order to promote international financial stability, improve the functioning of financial markets and reduce the tendency for financial shocks to propagate from country to country, and to enhance the institutional framework to support global financial stability. It is now apparent that the reforms that it has proposed, although important, have not been sufficient to avoid major global financial instability. If it is to become the main instrument for the formulation of reforms of the global financial system it must take into consideration the importance of financial stability for the development of the real economy. In addition it must increase the representation of developing countries to adequately reflect the views and conditions in these countries and be made accountable to a democratically representative institution such as the Global Economic Coordination Council proposed above.

The development of financial institutions that are too big to fail has played an important role in the development of the crisis and has made the resolution of the crisis both difficult and costly, both for taxpayers and for the global economy. It is imperative not only that is adequate oversight of these large institution but that efforts be made to limit their size and the extent of their interactions, to limit the scope of systemic risk. This will require more effective global cooperation in financial and competition regulation. Movement towards this goal might be enhanced by taking steps to lay the groundwork for a Global Financial Regulatory Authority and a Global Competition Authority. With so many firms operating across borders, it is difficult to rely on national regulatory authorities. There may be large externalities generated by the action (or inaction) of national authorities. A potential, but partial, remedy to this difficulty is the proposal for a College of Supervisors to oversee systemically relevant global financial institutions.

This could provide a basis for a more comprehensive Global Authority.

(f) Host Country regulation of foreign subsidiaries In the absence of adequate global coordination, financial sector regulation will need to be based on the host country, not the home country, and may entail requiring the establishment of subsidiaries, rather than relying on branches.

(g) Regulatory institutions

While inadequate regulations are partly to blame for the current crisis, in some cases good regulations were not effectively applied and enforced. This highlights the need for reforms in regulatory structures, including reforms that make the possibility of regulatory capture less likely. The weaker is the system of global regulation, the more segmented will financial markets have to be to ensure global stability.

7. Support for Financial Innovations to Enhance Risk Mitigation The absence of global systems of risk bearing and the absence of—and in some cases resistance to—innovations that would facilitate efficient risk bearing, such as GDP indexed bonds and mortgage products which better manage the risks associated with home ownership must be remedied. Governments and the international financial institutions need to explore meaningful innovations that would enhance risk management and distribution and how markets might be encouraged to do a better job. In particular, while there have been some expansion in capital markets in domestic currencies in developing countries, developing countries still bear the brunt of exchange and interest rate fluctuations. IFI lending in (possibly baskets of) lo-

cal currencies and the provision of exchange and interest rate cover might be important steps in improving international risk markets.

8. Mechanisms for handling Sovereign Debt Restructuring and Cross-border Investment Disputes There is an urgent need for renewed commitment to develop an equitable and generally acceptable Sovereign Debt Restructuring Mechanism, as a well as an improved framework for handling cross border bankruptcies. One way by which this might be done is through the creation of an independent structure, such as an International Bankruptcy Court. The United Nations Commission on International Trade Law provides a model that could be extended to the harmonization of national legislation on cross border disputes dealing with trade in financial services. A number of countries may face difficulties in meeting their external debt commitments as the crisis worsens and debt rescheduling becomes more and more difficult due to an increase in creditors not represented in the Paris Club. The current crisis has already seen a number of bankruptcies of companies that operate across national borders, and their number is likely to increase. The absence of a formal mechanism for dealing with the impact of cross border bankruptcy and insolvency, especially when related to financial institutions, transmits the adverse economic effects to the global economy.

It is especially important to achieve a uniform approach to financial and investment disputes on bankruptcy and insolvency, given the fact that the regulations dealing with these matters included in bilateral free trade agreements often transcend existing multilateral treaties and national legislation.

9. Completion of a Truly Development-Oriented Trade Round

There is a need for a true development round, to create an international trade regime which truly promotes growth in the developing countries. It is essential, that in all trade negotiations, the long recognized principle of special and differential treatment of developing countries be preserved.

10. More Stable and Sustainable Development Finance

The need for more and more stable sources of finance for development, including for the investments needed to address the long run challenges of responding to climate change, and new institutions for disbursement of funds. In the absence of better systems of risk mitigation, it is especially important for developing countries to be wary of measures that expose them to greater risk and volatility, such as capital market liberalization. Developing countries should use all the tools at their disposal, price interventions, quantitative restrictions, and prudential regulations, in order to help manage international capital flows.

Market-driven international capital flows are of a magnitude and volatility that they can offset any formal mechanism to provide additional finance for development. Thus, an active management of foreign capital inflows will be required to ensure that they are supportive of government counter-cyclical policies. The Articles of Agreement of the International Monetary Fund provided to members the facility of controlling capital inflows and expressly excluded the use of Fund resources to meet imbalances resulting from capital account disequilibrium. The Fund should thus be encouraged to return to its first principles and support countries that attempt to manage external flows in support domestic counter cyclical policy.

The international community needs to explore a variety of mechanisms of innovative finance, including regular emissions of a new global reserves (SDRs), revenues generated from the

auction of global natural resources (such as ocean fishing rights and pollution emission permits), and international taxes (such as a carbon tax, which would simultaneously help address problems of global warming, or a financial services tax, which would simultaneously help stabilize international financial markets.)

The receipts could be directed to support the developing countries costs of reducing greenhouse gas emissions in the context of their national policies to promote sustainable development. The effective implementation of national systems of taxation form a crucial part of domestic development finance. Measures must be taken to preserve national autonomy in the selection of the sources and methods of government financing while ensuring that national differences do not create incentives to evade responsibility of contributors to the support of government policies. An efficient method of achieving this result would be the acceptance by all countries of an amendment of Article 26 of the United Nations Model Double Taxation Convention between Developed and Developing Countries to make the exchange of information automatic.

IV. ISLAMIC FINANCE AND THE GLOBAL CRISIS

Internationally, Islamic banks appear to be more resilient to the global economic turndown and international financial crisis than conventional banks. They tend to avoid the speculative investments, such as derivatives, that many analysts believe led to the financial crisis affecting conventional banks. For many observers, Islamic Finance serves as a vehicle for recovering from the international financial crisis. The Islamic banking industry may be able to strengthen its position in the international market as investors and companies seek alternate sources of financing.

However, as Islamic banks operate within a global financial system, they have not been completely insulated from the recent economic and financial shocks. For instance, on the one hand, the Islamic financial industry is considered by many to be less risky because financial transactions are backed by physical assets. On the other hand, Islamic banks may be more vulnerable to fluctuations in the mortgage market, given their high activity in the real estate sector compared to conventional banks. The recent slowdown in real estate activity in the Gulf economies raises concerns about some Islamic banks' financial positions.

A. Performance of Islamic Bonds

A key segment of the Islamic Finance market is Islamic bonds, known as sukuk. The global market for Islamic bonds is estimated to be $80 billion currently. After increasing more than five-fold from 2004 to 2007, global issuance of sukuk hit a three-year low point in 2008 . Sales of new Islamic bonds amounted to $15.8 billion in 2008, compared to $46.7 billion in 2007.15 Corporate issuances represented about 60% of total new Islamic bonds issued in 2008, and sovereign and quasi-sovereign issues represented the remainder of new issuances. The bulk of sukuk issuance comes from Malaysia and the United Arab Emirates, although the Islamic bond market is widening. While the sukuk market is small in comparison to the market for conventional bonds, it was one of the world's fastest growing financial instruments prior to the recent slowdown. Sukuk issuance began slowing down in late 2008, partly due to the global economic turndown, The international sukuk market faced lower levels of liquidity, resulting from declines in oil prices and reduced confidence from investor. Additionally, global issuance of Islamic bonds may have slowed in 2008 due to concerns raised by the Accounting and Auditing Organization for Islamic Financial Institutions (AAOIFI) about thc shariah-compliance of some sukuks. Despite current challenges, many analysts believe that the long-term viability of the Islamic bond market appears strong, owing to the growing popularity of Islamic financial products, increased government interest in

Islamic Finance, investment and financing needs of the Gulf countries, and financial institution seeking greater diversification.

B. Steps Forward-- Some Recommendations

Islamic financial markets are operating far below their potential because Islamic banking by itself cannot take root in the absence of the other necessary components of an Islamic financial system. A number of limitations will have to be addressed before any long- term strategy can be formulated:

- A uniform regulatory and legal framework supportive of an Islamic financial system has not yet been developed. Existing banking regulations in Islamic countries are based on the Western banking model. Similarly, Islamic financial institutions face difficulties operating in non- Islamic countries owing to the absence of a regulatory body that operates in accordance with Islamic principles. The development of a regulatory and supervisory framework that would address the issues specific to Islamic institutions would further enhance the integration of Islamic markets and international financial markets.

- There is no single, sizable, and organized financial center that can claim to be functioning in accordance with Islamic principles. Although stock markets in emerging Islamic countries such as Egypt, Jordan, and Pakistan are active, they are not fully compatible with Islamic principles. The stock markets in Iran and

Sudan may come closest to operating in compliance with Islamic principles. Moreover, the secondary market for Islamic products is extremely shallow and illiquid, and money markets are almost nonexistent, since viable instruments are not currently available. The development of an interbank market is another challenge.

- The pace of innovation is slow. For years, the market has offered the same traditional instruments geared toward shortand medium- term maturities, but it has not yet come up with the necessary instruments to handle maturities at the extremes. There is a need for risk-management tools to equip clients with instruments to hedge against the high volatility in currency and commodities markets. In addition, the market lacks the necessary instruments to provide viable alternatives for public debt financing.

- An Islamic financial system needs sound accounting procedures and standards. Western accounting procedures are not adequate because of the different nature and treatment of financial instruments. Well-defined procedures and standards are crucial for information disclosure, building investors' confidence, and monitoring and surveillance. Proper standards will also help the integration of Islamic financial markets with international markets. Islamic institutions have a shortage of trained personnel who can analyze and manage portfolios, and develop innovative products according to Islamic financial principles. Only a limited number of Islamic institutions can afford to train their staffs and deploy resources in product development.

- There is lack of uniformity in the religious principles applied in Islamic countries. In the absence of a universally accepted central religious authority, Islamic banks have formed their own religious boards for guidance. Islamic banks have to consult their respective religious boards, or shariah advisors, to seek approval for each new instrument. Differences in interpretation of Islamic principles by different schools of thought may mean that identical financial instruments are rejected by one board but accepted by another. Thus, the same instrument may not be acceptable in all countries. This problem can be addressed by forming a uniform council representing different schools of thought to define cohesive rules and to expedite the process of introducing new products.

Improvement can be made in several areas to promote and enhance the providing Islamic financial services. However, certain areas deserve immediate attention.

1. Financial Engineering:

Financial engineering and financial innovations are driving the global financial system toward greater economic efficiency by expanding the opportunities for sharing risk, lowering transaction costs, and reducing asymmetric information and agency costs. Financial engineering involves the design, development, and implementation of innovative financial instruments and processes as well as the formulation of creative solutions. Financial engineering may lead to a new consumer-type financial instrument, or a new security, or a new process or creative solution to corporate finance problems, such as the need to lower funding costs, manage risk better, or increase the return on investments.

For Islamic financial institutions, a financial engineering challenge is to introduce new Shariah-compatible products that enhance liquidity, risk management, and portfolio diversification. Generally, attempts to apply financial engineering techniques to Islamic banking will require committing a great deal of resources to understanding the risk-return characteristics of each building block of the system and offering new products with different risk-return profiles that meet the demand of investors, financial intermediaries, and entrepreneurs for liquidity and safety. Securitization is a prime candidate for financial engineering. New financial innovations are also needed to satisfy the demand for instruments at both ends of the maturity structure: extremely short-term deposits and long-term investments. Money markets that are Shariah compatible do not exist at present, and there is no equivalent of an Islamic interbank market where banks could place, say, overnight funds or could borrow to satisfy a need for temporary liquidity. Although securitization of a pool of lease portfolios could help to develop the interbank market, the volume of transactions offered by securitization may not be sufficient to meet the demand.

Islamic financial institutions are, in general, of small size and cannot afford to invest substantial funds in research and development. They are unable to reap the benefits of economies Informal discussions with practitioners revealed that religious boards sometimes are extremely rigid on minor technical matters and make the process of introducing a new product difficult and lengthy, resulting in missed business opportunities. The importance of financial engineering, Islamic financial institutions should seriously consider making joint efforts to develop the basic infrastructure for introducing new products. Conducting basic research and development collectively may save some of the costs required to build this infrastructure individually. A good example of such collective effort would be to sponsor research in the development of analytical models, computer systems, and tools to analyze the risk and return on different instruments.

Financial engineering is an area where Islamic financial institutions could benefit from more experienced Western institutions, which are more sophisticated in engineering and marketing the right product to the right client. Conventional investment banks, which have invested heavily in the infrastructure for developing new products, can work for or with Islamic financial institutions to develop Shariah- compliant products.

2. Risk Management and Diversification:

Due to limited resources, Islamic banks are often unable to afford high-cost management information systems or the technology to assess and monitor risk in a timely fashion. With weak management and lack of proper risk-monitoring systems, the risk exposure of Islamic banks is high.

Providing a more diverse mix of financial services or spreading risks over a larger geographic area imply at least the potential for improved diversification, so the same protection against financial distress can be attained with fewer resources. For Islamic financial institutions, geographic expansion of the depositor base could achieve diversification on the liabilities side. Diversification on the assets side could reduce the variance of the returns that accrue to claimholders of the financial intermediary. Also, geographic and sectoral diversification on the assets side could break up the financial institutions' concentration in a region or a sector and thus reduce its exposure by creating less perfectly correlated risks. Geographic spread of products can further help the financial intermediary to improve its credit risk by selecting borrowers with the best credit and avoiding those with the weakest. With diversification, Islamic banks would be able to extend the maturity frontier.

Islamic financial intermediaries need to adopt appropriate risk management not only for their own portfolio but also for that of their clients. Diversification and risk management are closely associated with the degree of market incompleteness. In highly incomplete markets, financial intermediaries are in a better position to provide diversification and risk management for the client because the responsibility for risk diversification shifts from the investors to the financial intermediary, which is considered to be better at providing intertemporal risk management. Islamic financial institutions need to take immediate steps to devise an infrastructure for implementing proper measures, controls, and management of risk and to create innovative instruments to share, transfer, and mitigate financial risk so that entrepreneurs can concentrate on what they do best: managing exposure to business risk in which they have a comparative advantage.

Finally, Islamic financial institutions need to realize the importance not only of financial risk and its management but also of operational risk, which is risk due to the failure of controls and processes. Currently, there is a serious lack of a risk culture and of enterprise- level sponsorship of active risk management.

3. Non-Bank Financial Services:

For further growth, the role of intermediation should be extended beyond its traditional setup. In particular, there is a need to broaden the scope and range of financial services offered, similar to the concept of a "financial products supermarket." Such a supermarket would act like an "all-in-bank" covering all sorts of financial services. In this role, the Islamic bank would serve as a one-stop shop catering to different types of customers, ranging from private individuals, institutions, high-net-worth individuals, and corporations and offering products that serve their investment, borrowing, risk management, and wealth management needs. For example, such an institution would serve retail customers, manage investment portfolios, and provide various services for corporate customers. At the same time, like a broker, the financial products supermarket would be a retail firm that manages assets and offers payment and settlement services. Most Islamic banks are not adequately equipped to provide typical investment banking services, such as underwriting, guarantees, market research, and fee-based advisory services. The refinement and development of fee-based services would enhance the functionality of Islamic financial services. Fee-based contracts like joalah, wakalah, and kifalah require further development if they are to be recognized and operationalized to exploit the full capabilities of Islamic banks.

4. Development of Capital Markets:

Responding to the current wave of oil revenues and growing demand for Shariah-compliant products, Islamic capital markets are expanding at a quickening pace, and stakeholders are starting to realize their potential. Development of institutional infrastructure, such as accounting standards and regulatory bodies, is a step in the right direction. However, the market needs host governments to undertake strong leadership and constructive policy actions.

Well-developed Islamic capital markets will not only benefit borrowers and institutional investors, they also can enhance the stability of Islamic banks, providing them with improved portfolio, liquidity, and risk management tools. Ultimately, these developments will help to integrate Islamic financial markets, as well as the institutions that form them, into the broader conventional international financial system.

On the supply side, the volume of Islamic investments, with a preference for Shariah-compliant instruments, has grown to form a critical mass that can support a well-functioning and efficient capital market. It is evolving into a truly international market. Not only highly rated borrowers, such as the multilateral development banks (for example, the World Bank), but also developing-country borrowers with lower credit ratings, such as Pakistan, have successfully raised a considerable volume of funds in this market.

These institutions include the IFSB, AAOIFI, Liquidity Management Center, International Islamic Financial Markets, and International Islamic Rating Agency. On the demand side, countries in the developing world, especially the middle-income countries, will require a significant volume of investments in infrastructure over the next decade. For Indonesia alone, additional infrastructure investments of $5 billion (2 percent of GDP) are required annually, to reach a 6 percent medium-term growth target . Because the domestic capital markets of these borrowers are often too shallow to satisfy their large investment needs, they will have to access external sources of financing.

Furthermore, Muslim stakeholders in middle-income countries are increasingly expressing their preference for Shariah-compliant financing. In turn, financial intermediaries, including private sector commercial and investment banks, as well as development finance institutions, will have to start paying more attention to the "non- financial" needs of their clients.

For the multilateral development banks, the development of Islamic capital markets is a highly relevant topic. First, multilateral development banks are deeply involved in infrastructure finance and are naturally interested in the

Islamic capital market as a new and alternative source of financing. Second, by channeling the funds available in Islamic financial markets, which are mostly based in the countries with high savings such as the Gulf Cooperation Council countries and Malaysia, to finance investments in developing countries, multilateral development banks can create a new model for international cooperation while responding to the stakeholders' voices on both sides. Third, multilateral development banks can promote financial stability by encouraging the development of Islamic capital markets and providing the momentum to integrate the Islamic financial markets into the international financial system.

In the near future, structures such as ijarah (a lease) and murabahah (a cost-plus sales contract used to purchase commodities) that provide investors with a predetermined return as well as full recourse to the obligor probably will have more market potential than other structures. This will be driven primarily by investor preferences, but a large proportion of potential borrowers will prefer to lock in their borrowing costs rather than engage in pure profit-sharing schemes.

While the future appears promising, certain obstacles lie ahead, and market participants and regulators need to take concrete steps to support market takeoff. First and most important, market development requires strong sponsorship and leadership on the part of the host-country government, especially regarding legal and regulatory issues. For example, for an ijarah transaction, the owner of operating assets enters into a leasing transaction. While the owner of operating assets is often the government itself or related public sector bodies, the relevant laws and regulations in the host country may not allow these bodies to pledge or lease assets needed to structure an ijarah transaction. This is a fundamental point; the host country's policy actions are a key prerequisite for further market development.

In addition, borrowers, investors, and intermediaries need to nurture the market patiently. Islamic transactions are often less cost- efficient than conventional bond issues. Each new issue incurs higher legal and documentary expenses as well as distribution costs because it involves examining structural robustness in addition to evaluating the credit quality of the obligor. Since the terms available in Islamic capital markets are derived mostly from pricing levels in the more liquid conventional bond markets, there is no inherent cost advantage for borrowers tapping Islamic markets. Borrowers, therefore, need to formulate a comprehensive, long- term, and strategic view on how to reduce the overall cost of tapping Islamic markets, rather than focus on a single transaction. Investors can support market development by expressing their preference for Shariah-compliant instruments, namely, in their bid prices. Intermediaries can lead the process, perhaps through further standardization of transaction schemes and instruments.

V. THE GLOBAL FINANCIAL CRISIS: LESSONS FROM AND FOR ISLAMIC FINANCE

The problem, however, is that Islamic Finance is still in its infancy and commands a very small proportion of international finance. In addition, it does not genuinely reflect the ethos of Islamic teachings. The use of equity and PLS is still very small while that of debt- creating modes is preponderant. Moreover, even in the case of debt-creating modes, all the conditions laid down by the Shari'ah are not being faithfully observed by the use of legal stratagems (hiyal). This is partially due to a lack of proper understanding of the ultimate objective of Islamic Finance, the non-availability of trained personnel, and the absence of a number of shared or support institutions that are needed to minimize the risks associated with anonymity, moral hazard, principal/agent conflict of interest, and late settlement of financial obligations . In addition, consumerism has also been rapidly expanding in Muslim countries and promoting living beyond means. Financial institutions exploit this tendency to expand credit to raise their income. In addition there is a great deal of corruption in government finances which, along with inefficiency and wasteful spending, has led to high levels of budgetary deficits, which are financed by domestic as well as external borrowing.

In light of the financial crisis, some lessons of utmost significance can be derived from Islamic Finance and banking:-

1. There is deep-seated confidence in the correctness of Islamic Finance in terms of its adherence to funding by sales, leases, and partnerships, and in terms of its avoidance of loans of all types, given that they are a method of finance that takes finance away from the real market of production and exchange. Likewise, there is ingrained confidence in the principle of rejection of circulation or securitization of debts. These are the most important guarantees that a financial system will not slip into a crisis.

2. It is necessary to stop the attempts aiming at imitating the Western forms and practices of finance, which are devoid of the reality of goods, particularly those contracts that produce no added value but only result in shifting wealth from one hand to another. The point is that these contracts belong to the type of contracts whose total equals zero, including the so-called funds of Islamic caution, contracts of compound promises, imaginary contracts of investment, and other nominal practices that are founded upon no real production or exchange.

3. It is necessary to reevaluate certain financial dealings adopted by some Islamic banks — namely, those dealings that separate finance from the real market and avoid relying on the production of an added value. These dealings

rely on the accumulation of debts that are not accompanied by any movement in services and goods. Such dealings do not effect generation of wealth; they widen the gap between the real market and the financial market and contribute to inflation of debts in a way that leads to financial instability.

4. Also, the debts that are not based on real exchange of goods (but rather on overlapping contracts) result in illusory financial accumulations not reflecting the true identity and goal of Islamic Finance. As a consequence, Islamic Finance would fail to maintain its moral purity and would fail to apply its moral standards to the measures it follows. Here, one may make special mention of the transactions of tawarruq and murabahah for local and international commodities.

5. There is a need for reviewing the systems of financial markets in Muslim countries, with the aim of limiting financial speculations by laying down restrictions on their different types and also by banning the transactions that do not involve real investment. It is to be known that the systems applied in some Arab and Muslim markets do not allow many derivatives, which is one of the most important causes of the crisis.

6. It is necessary to revise many views and opinions, especially those practices falsely labeled "Islamic," such as the so-called short-term sale, derivatives and dealings on the same day, markets of caution, mudawalat (speculations) via the Internet using currency, and so forth. These practices facilitate the prevalence of the mentality of quick profit

and encourage — albeit implicitly — the spirit of selfishness and financial speculations that do not increase production or create any added value.

7. Principles of Islamic Finance should be presented to the world as part and parcel of the true image of Islam, whose message is directed to all humankind — a mercy for the worlds. These principles are not specific to Muslims; they are principles of Islam, which is a universal religion. In fact, throughout the ages, these principles have always been known and practiced in all communities in their exchanges and transactions, though some financial dealings and speculations have marred them. Above all, these Islamic principles are required by the scientific, logical analyses of economic and financial systems and by the principles of human rights, notably the right to reaping the fruits of one's own property and the right to protection against encroachment upon the personal property of those benefiting from funding. This is the meaning of justice and elimination of oppression. It is the meaning that is constantly stressed by all the rulings and branches of Islamic Shari`ah.

8. There is a need for reevaluating — from the perspective of Islamic Shari`ah — the current systems of Islamic sukuk (financial documents), in an attempt to perfect their rules and lay down organizational and jurisprudential regulations that would ensure they will not slip into the forms of securitization that dominated the Western financial markets.

9. From the standpoint of Islamic Finance, a firm stance should be taken against selling debts (a practice found in

Malaysia) and against discounting and rescheduling them, even under false names.

Future directions

The further growth and development of the Islamic financial system will depend largely on the nature of innovations introduced in the market. The immediate need is to deploy human and financial resources to develop instruments to enhance liquidity;

develop secondary, money, and interbank markets; perform asset/liability and risk management; and introduce public finance instruments. The Islamic financial system can also offer alternatives at the microfinance level.

Securitization is a step in the right direction but even this requires more sophistication. The scope of securitization —the process of unbundling and repackaging a financial asset to enhance its mar- ketability, negotiability, and liquidity—in Islamic financial markets is very promising, because current market operations are restricted by the dearth of liquidity-enhancing products; secondary markets lack depth and breadth; and, more important, instruments for asset/liability management are simply nonexistent. With the expansion of securitization, the customer base of Islamic financial systems will grow as institutional investors, who have access to broader maturity structures, are attracted to the market;

the secondary market will develop; and asset/liability management will become a reality. Other strong candidates for securitization include real estate, leasing, and trade receivables because of the collateralized nature of their cash flows.

Microfinance is another candidate for the application of Islamic Finance. Islamic Finance promotes entrepreneurship and risk sharing, and its expansion to the poor could be an effective development tool. The social benefits are obvious, since the poor currently are often exploited by lenders charging usurious rates.

An Islamic financial system can play a vital role in the economic development of Islamic countries by mobilizing dormant savings that are being intentionally kept out of interest-based financial channels and by facilitating the development of capital markets. At the same time, the development of such systems would enable savers and borrowers to choose financial instruments compatible with their business needs, social values, and religious beliefs

REFERENCES

1. Abbas Mirakhor, Islamic Finance and Globalization: A Convergence? Journal of Islamic Economics, Banking and Finance (Jiebf) ,Volume - 3, Number - 2, July - December 2007.

2. Al Ghannam, Mohamed,29. May 2009,the Financial Crisis & The Future of the Egyptian Economy, Online at Http://Mpra.Ub.Uni- Muenchen .De/15474/

3. Allen & Overy Llp, 25 February 2009,Islamic Microfinance Report.

4. IMF. (2008). World Economic Outlook Database, October 2008.

5. IMF. (2009). World Economic Outlook Database, April 2009.

6. IMF. (2009). Global Economic Slump Challenges Policies, World Economic Outlook Update, January 28, 2009.

7. Mervyn K Lewis.(2008).In What Ways Does Islamic Banking Differ from Conventional Finance?, Journal of Islamic Economics, Banking and Finance (Jiebf) ,Volume - 4, Number - 3, September - December 2008.

8. Monzer Kahf ,the Global Financial Crisis:Ideas for Long Term Solutions: Short Notes,Translated by Dr. Ahmed El-gharbawy .At:Http://Www.Islamonline.Net.

9. Organisation of the Islamic Conference Statistical,Economic and Social Research and Training Centre for Islamic Countries (Sesric) , the Current Global Financial Crisis, Monthly Reports, M a Y 2 0 0 9.

10. Robert J. Shiller.(2008) . The Subprime Solution: How Today's Global Financial Crisis Happened and What to Do about It (Princeton, Nj: Princeton University Press).

11. Shayerah Ilias .(2009). Islamic Finance: Overview and Policy Concerns, Congressional Research Service, February 9, 2009.

12. Sarah s. al-rifaee ,Islamic banking myths and Facts.At:Www.Arabinsight.Org 13. the Commission of Experts on Reforms of the International monetary and financial system Recommendations,19 march 2009 at : Http:// Www.Un.Org/Ga/President/63/Letters/Recommendationexperts2003 09.Pdf.

14. Umer Chapra.(2009).The Global Financial Crisis Some Suggestions for Reform of the Global Financial Architecture in the Light of Islamic Finance, Center for Islamic Area Studies at Kyoto University (Kias),Japan , June 2009.

15. Umer Chapra.(2008). The Global Financial Crisis: Can Islamic Finance Help Minimize the Severity and Frequency of Such a Crisis in the Future?, A Paper Prepared for Presentation at the Forum on the Global Financial Crisis to Be Held at the Islamic Development Bank on 25 October 2008.

16. UNCTAD. (2009). Global Economic Crisis: Implications for Trade and Development, Trade and Development